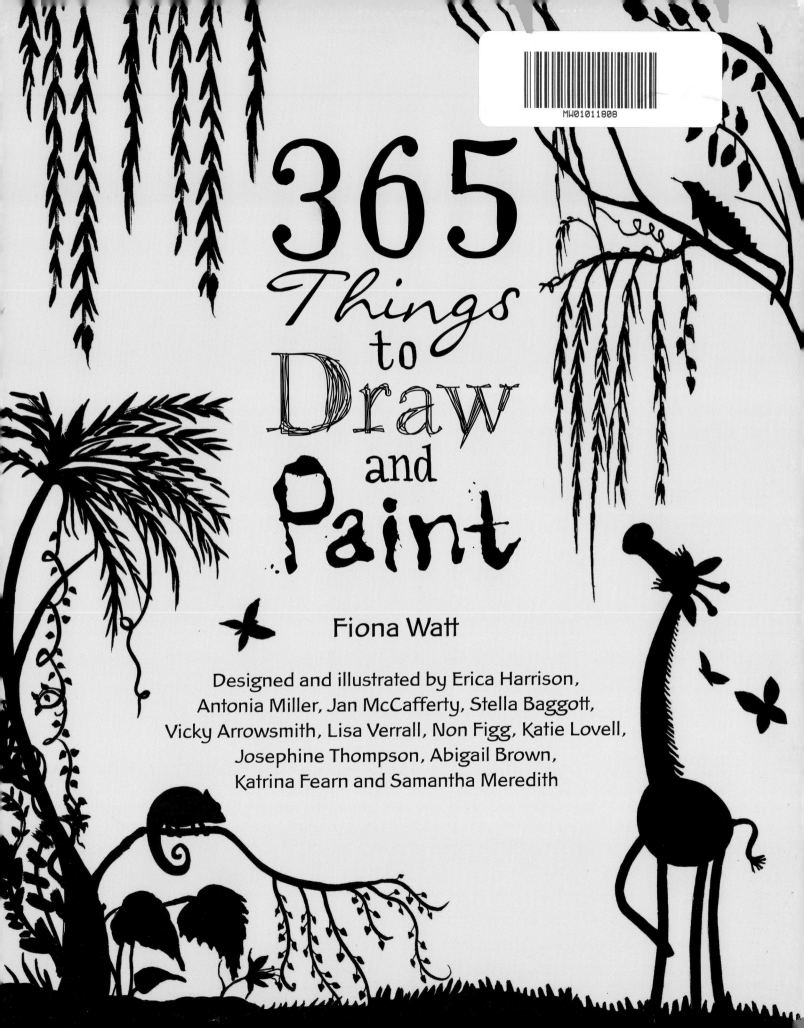

365
Things
to
Draw
and
Paint

Fiona Watt

Designed and illustrated by Erica Harrison,
Antonia Miller, Jan McCafferty, Stella Baggott,
Vicky Arrowsmith, Lisa Verrall, Non Figg, Katie Lovell,
Josephine Thompson, Abigail Brown,
Katrina Fearn and Samantha Meredith

About this book

This book is full of ideas for things to draw and paint. You'll find simple step-by-step instructions showing you what to do, as well as lots of ideas for drawing or painting other things using the same technique.

154 Collage robot - page 50

Contents

316 Draw a lion - page 109

185 Paint tropical birds - page 62

313 Draw a leopard - page 108

177 Print an owl - page 59

165 Make a bug - page 54

112 Draw sportsmen - page 36

320 Draw a football crowd - page 112

Drawing dogs

1 Simple dog

Use a yellow pencil to draw ovals for a dog's head and body. Then, add a neck and ears. Draw thin legs and a tail. Then, use a black pencil to add eyes, a nose and a mouth. Draw a collar, too.

2 Hairy dog

Scribble up and down to draw a hairy dog's body. Then, draw little zigzags for fuzzy ears and a tail. Add legs and paws, then draw its eyes, nose and mouth with a felt-tip pen.

3 Poodle

Draw a shape for a poodle's head and snout. Then, scribble around and around for the body. Add scribbly ears and a tail, then draw the legs. Add eyes, a nose and a mouth with a black felt-tip pen.

4 Sitting dog

Draw an oval for the dog's head, then draw lots of looping lines for the muzzle. Draw the body beneath the head. Then, add paws, a tail and ears. Use a felt-tip pen to draw eyes, a mouth and a big triangular nose.

4

Copy the ideas on this page to draw lots of different dogs or create some of your own.

5 Howling dog

Draw the dog's head looking up and add a round mouth.

6 Add a bone

Draw part of a bone on either side of a dog's mouth.

Add a coat.

7 Long fur

Draw lots of very long lines for a dog with long fur.

8 Running dog

Draw the legs stretched out in front and behind the body.

9 Wagging tail

Draw little curved lines beside a dog's tail to make it look as if it's moving.

10 Fast asleep

Draw 'U' shapes for the eyes of a sleeping dog.

Shark attack

11 **Shark stencil**

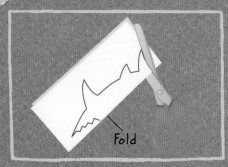

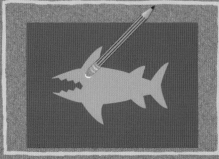

1. To make a stencil, fold a square of thick paper in half. Draw the outline of half a shark against the fold. Then, cut out the shark, but don't cut along the fold.

2. Unfold the stencil and lay it on blue paper. Spread pale blue paint on an old plate. Then, dip a sponge into the paint and dab it again and again over the hole in the stencil.

3. Let the paint dry. Squeeze thick white paint onto the plate. Using the eraser on the end of a pencil, print an eye. Paint a black pupil and eyebrow with a thin brush.

12

Fish

Cut smaller stencils to print lots of little fish around your shark.

Big picture
Make a big picture with lots of sharks and fish swimming around.

14

Bubbles
Print bubbles with an eraser on the end of a pencil.

Printed city

15 Train

Dip the eraser into the paint for each print.

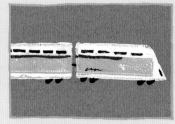

1. Dip the side of an eraser into white paint and use it to print the train. Then, cut a piece off one end and print the engine.

2. When the paint is dry, use the side of the eraser to print a blue stripe on top of each white shape. Let the paint dry.

3. Use a thin black felt-tip pen to draw windows and wheels. Then, use a chalk pastel or chalk to draw red stripes along the side.

This road and the river were painted on the background.

Draw markings on a road with white chalk.

16 Boat

Cut a diagonal piece off both ends of an eraser and print the bottom of a boat. Print the top with the side of two different erasers.

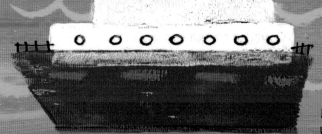

Draw portholes and railings with a thin black pen.

Cut one end off
an eraser to make
a slanting roof.

(17) Buildings

Use different sizes
of erasers to print
buildings. Draw
windows when
the paint is dry.

You could draw a
railway track and
some signals.

(18) Car

1. Dip the side of an eraser
into paint and use it to
print the body of the car.
Let the paint dry.

2. Draw the roof with chalk
or a chalk pastel. Then,
add windows and wheels
with a thin black pen.

Textured papers

You can paint your own textured papers to use in pictures and collages. Experiment with some of the ideas shown on the butterflies on these pages.

To make a butterfly, cut out wings and a body from two pieces of textured paper. Then, glue them onto another piece of paper.

Splattering creates dots of different sizes.

This red butterfly was dry brushed.

21 **Layering**

Paint one layer of paint and let it dry. Then, brush another layer of paint on top.

19 **Splattering**

Dip a brush into runny paint and hold it over some paper. Pull your finger back over the bristles to flick spots of paint onto the paper.

20 **Dry brush**

Don't use water.

Dip a dry brush with coarse bristles into thick paint. Brush stripes of paint across your paper.

This pink butterfly is made from splattered paper.

Fingerprinted spots

Wax resist scribbles

22 **Wax resist**

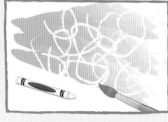

Draw patterns on thick white paper with a wax crayon. Then, brush watery paint over the top.

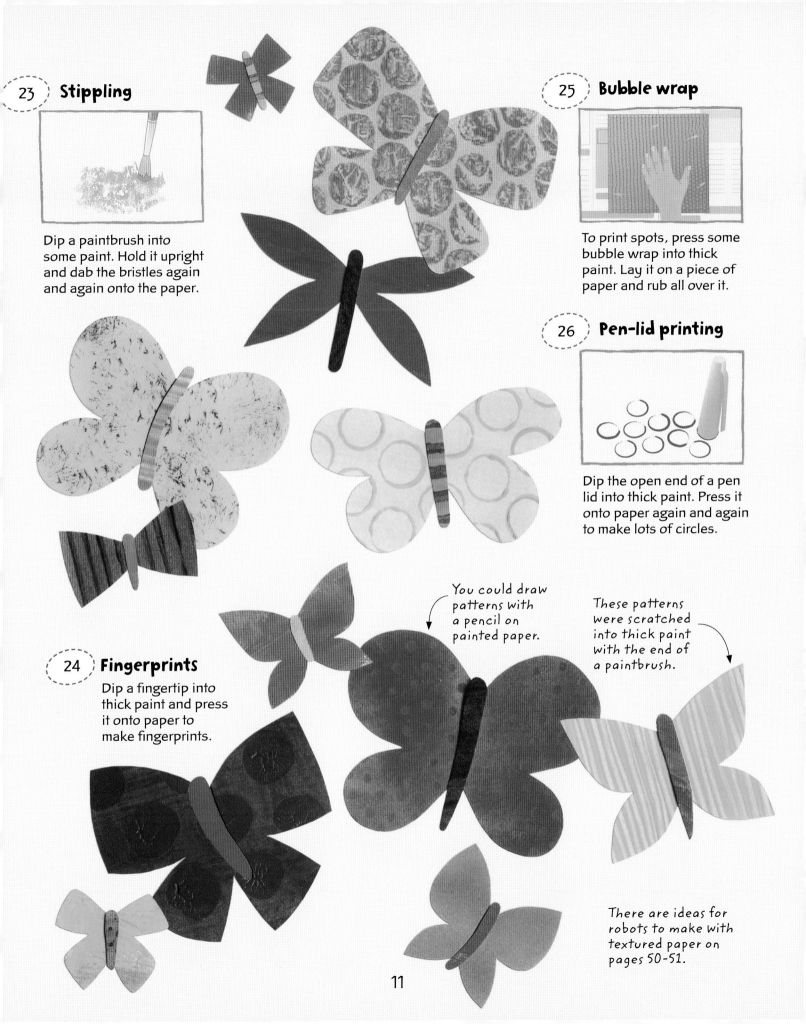

23 Stippling

Dip a paintbrush into some paint. Hold it upright and dab the bristles again and again onto the paper.

24 Fingerprints

Dip a fingertip into thick paint and press it onto paper to make fingerprints.

25 Bubble wrap

To print spots, press some bubble wrap into thick paint. Lay it on a piece of paper and rub all over it.

26 Pen-lid printing

Dip the open end of a pen lid into thick paint. Press it onto paper again and again to make lots of circles.

You could draw patterns with a pencil on painted paper.

These patterns were scratched into thick paint with the end of a paintbrush.

There are ideas for robots to make with textured paper on pages 50-51.

Painted chalets

27

Press gently as you draw.

1. On thick paper, draw a ski chalet with some steps. Then, add pointed shapes for hills, and curved lines for mountains.

2. Paint the sky and hills with pale blue watery paints. Let the paint dry, then paint the sky again to make it darker.

3. Paint different parts of the chalet with pale paints. Let each patch of paint dry before painting the next one.

4. Add details, such as shutters and a balcony, with a thin brush. When all the paint has dried, draw details with pencils.

28 **Stars and smoke**
Use chalks to add smoke from the chimneys and stars in the sky.

You could paint a woodshed beside a chalet.

29 Tracks in the snow

Use chalk or a pencil to draw tracks that a skier has made.

30 Pine trees

Draw trees and fill them with different shades of paint. Add the trunks when the paint is dry.

31 Window boxes

Use a thin paintbrush to add window boxes with bright flowers.

You could add a pile of chopped logs.

This path winding between the chalets was painted with watery blue paint.

13

Mixing paints

If you don't have the shade of paint that you want to use, find out on these pages how you can mix it using other paints.

Mix red and yellow to make orange.

Mix red, yellow and blue to make brown.

Mix blue and yellow to make green.

Mix red and blue to make purple.

(32) Poppies

1. Mix some watery orange paint. Then, paint a large, wet blob on a piece of thick paper.

2. Hold the piece of paper at an angle so that the paint runs down in a line to make a stalk.

3. Paint several more poppies in the same way. Don't worry if the paints bleed together.

4. Paint some extra stalks between the poppies. When the paint is dry, use chalk to add the middles.

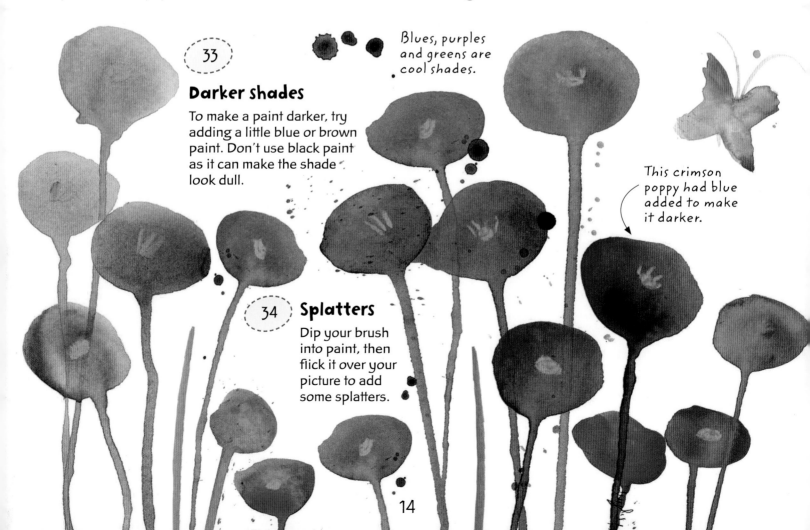

(33)

Blues, purples and greens are cool shades.

Darker shades

To make a paint darker, try adding a little blue or brown paint. Don't use black paint as it can make the shade look dull.

This crimson poppy had blue added to make it darker.

(34) **Splatters**

Dip your brush into paint, then flick it over your picture to add some splatters.

14

35

Lighter shades

You can add white paint to lighten a shade, or add water to make it 'thinner'.

These two butterflies were painted with the same paint...

... but this one had water added to the paint to make it paler.

36

Butterflies

Paint some butterflies fluttering above the poppies. Use a chalk pastel to make markings on the wings.

Reds, yellows and oranges are warm shades.

Dotted painting

37 **Turtle**

Use a white pencil.

1. Draw an oval for a turtle's shell on black paper. Then, draw some more ovals on the shell. Add four flippers, a head and tail.

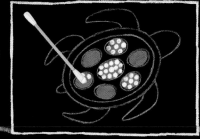

2. Fill in the small ovals with green paint, let the paint dry. Dip a cotton bud (in US = Q-tip) into white paint and use it to print dots on some of the ovals.

3. Fill all the shapes with printed dots. When the paint has dried, paint two larger circles for eyes and add black dots for the pupils.

For a background like this, draw wavy lines across the paper and fill the shapes with printed dots.

38 **Kangaroo**

Draw a simple outline for the body and head, then draw lines to divide the shapes into sections.

39 Crab

Draw a crab with four pairs of back legs, and two large pincers.

40 Lizard

Draw a lizard with a white pencil and add lines on its tail. Decorate each section.

41 Platypus

Decorate a platypus with lots of dots. Paint the head and bill, and draw crisscrossed lines on its tail.

42 Fish

Draw an outline of a fish. Divide the body with white lines and fill the shapes with dots.

43 Snake

Draw a long, wavy shape for a snake's body. Add a head and tongue.

Scribbly bugs

44 **Beetle**

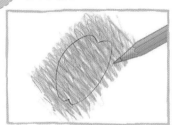   

Use a thin pen.

1. Draw the outline of a body. Then, scribble all over it with different green and blue pencils.

2. Then, draw the top part of the body and scribble over it with red and blue pencils. Cut out the shapes.

3. Draw a large leaf on another piece of paper Then, glue the bug's body parts on top.

4. Cut out two eyes and glue them on. Draw dots in the eyes, feelers on the head, then add six legs.

45 **Make a picture**

Draw lots of scribbly leaves and flowers, then add different bugs on top.

47 **Ant**

To make an ant, cut out a head, and two more pieces for the body.

46

Snail

Scribble the lines for a snail's body with different shades of red pencils. Draw a spiral on a blue shell.

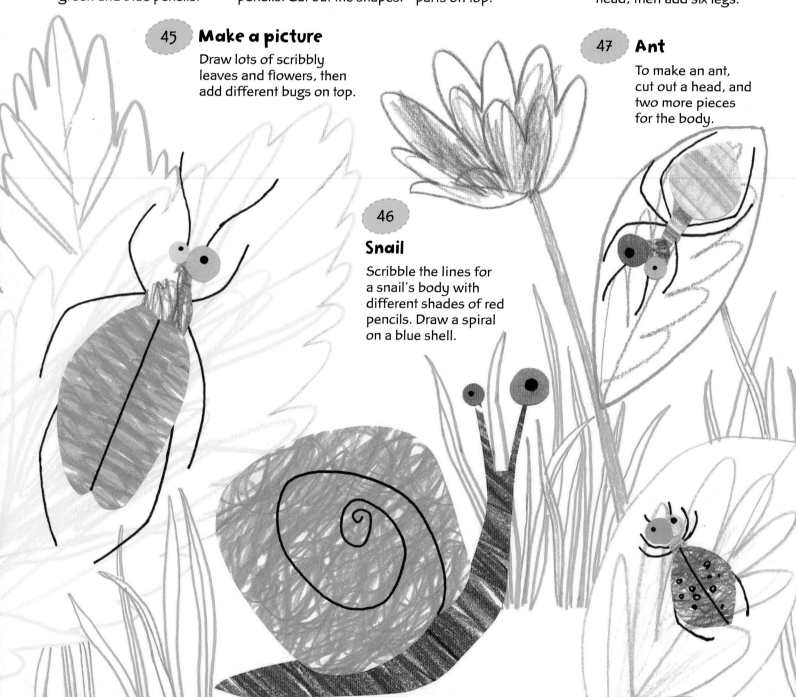

48 Butterfly

Cut out a body and
wings from scribbly
paper. Add eyes,
then use pens to draw
patterns on the wings.

Scribble a
cloud with a
blue pencil.

49 Bee

Use pale pencils to
scribble patterns
for the wings. Add
stripes on the body.

This fly's body
was filled
in with lots
of different
pencils.

Fill a flower
with lots
of scribbly
lines.

You could
draw a
worm.

Fingerprinted monkeys

50 Simple monkey

This is for the bottom part of the head.

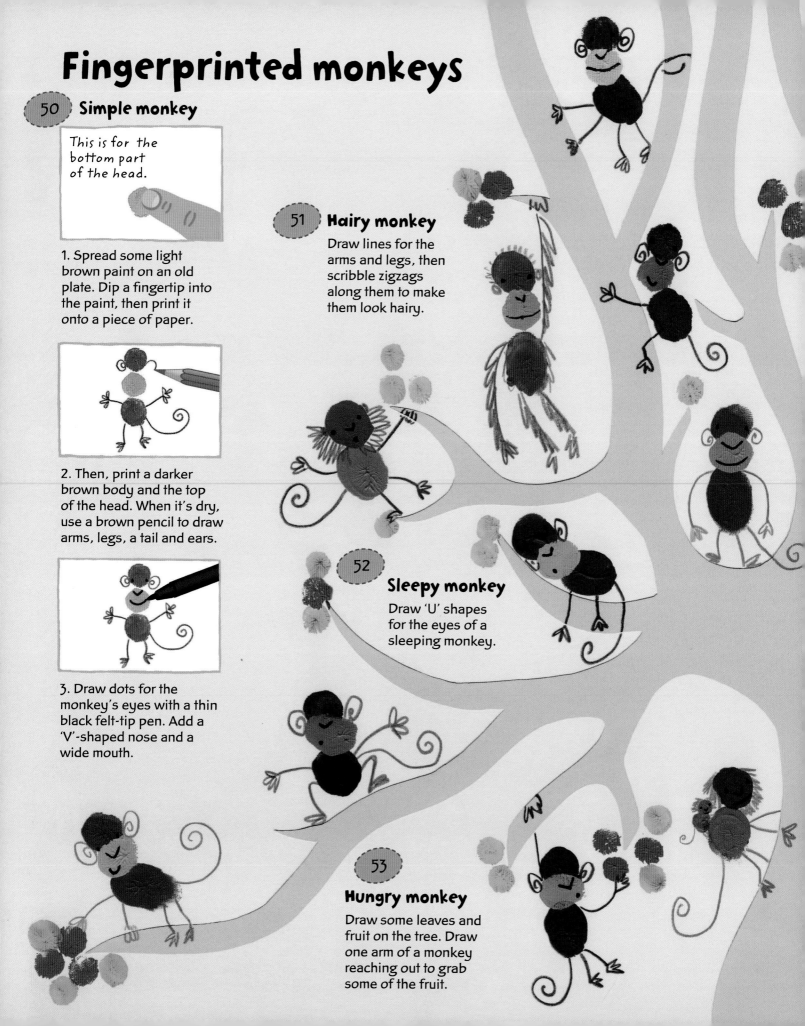

1. Spread some light brown paint on an old plate. Dip a fingertip into the paint, then print it onto a piece of paper.

2. Then, print a darker brown body and the top of the head. When it's dry, use a brown pencil to draw arms, legs, a tail and ears.

3. Draw dots for the monkey's eyes with a thin black felt-tip pen. Add a 'V'-shaped nose and a wide mouth.

51 Hairy monkey

Draw lines for the arms and legs, then scribble zigzags along them to make them look hairy.

52 Sleepy monkey

Draw 'U' shapes for the eyes of a sleeping monkey.

53 Hungry monkey

Draw some leaves and fruit on the tree. Draw one arm of a monkey reaching out to grab some of the fruit.

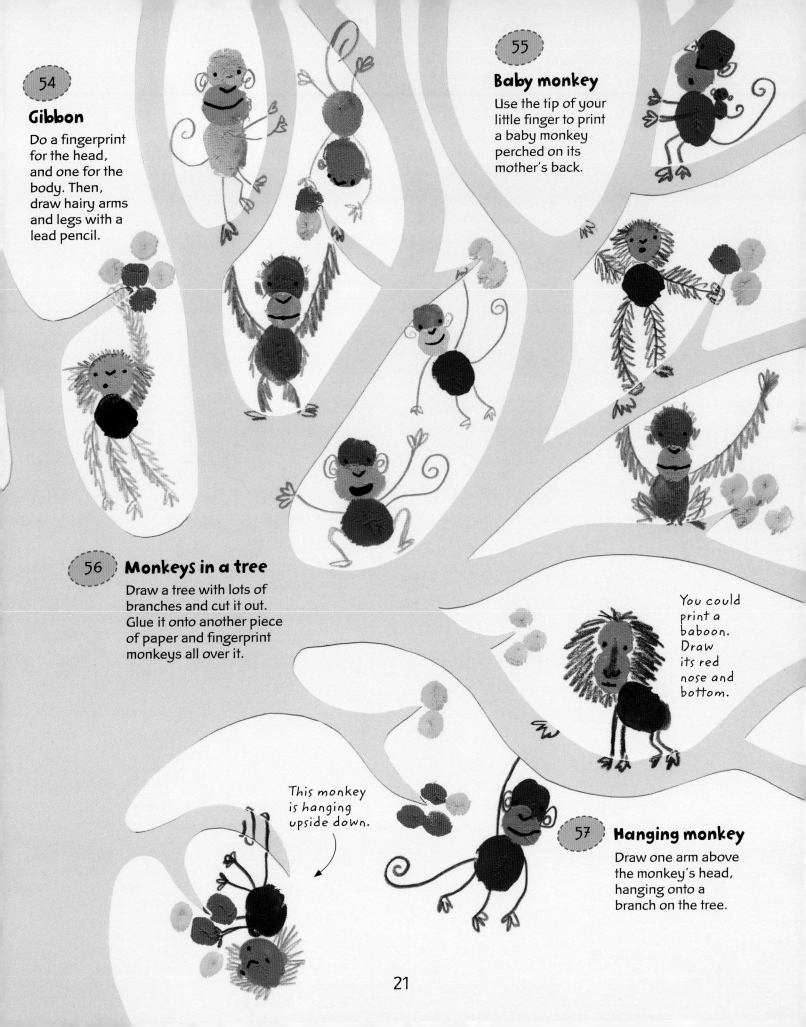

54

Gibbon

Do a fingerprint for the head, and one for the body. Then, draw hairy arms and legs with a lead pencil.

55

Baby monkey

Use the tip of your little finger to print a baby monkey perched on its mother's back.

56 ## Monkeys in a tree

Draw a tree with lots of branches and cut it out. Glue it onto another piece of paper and fingerprint monkeys all over it.

You could print a baboon. Draw its red nose and bottom.

This monkey is hanging upside down.

57 ## Hanging monkey

Draw one arm above the monkey's head, hanging onto a branch on the tree.

Draw a hand

Use a pen to draw around your hand on a piece of paper, then use the ideas on these pages to decorate it.

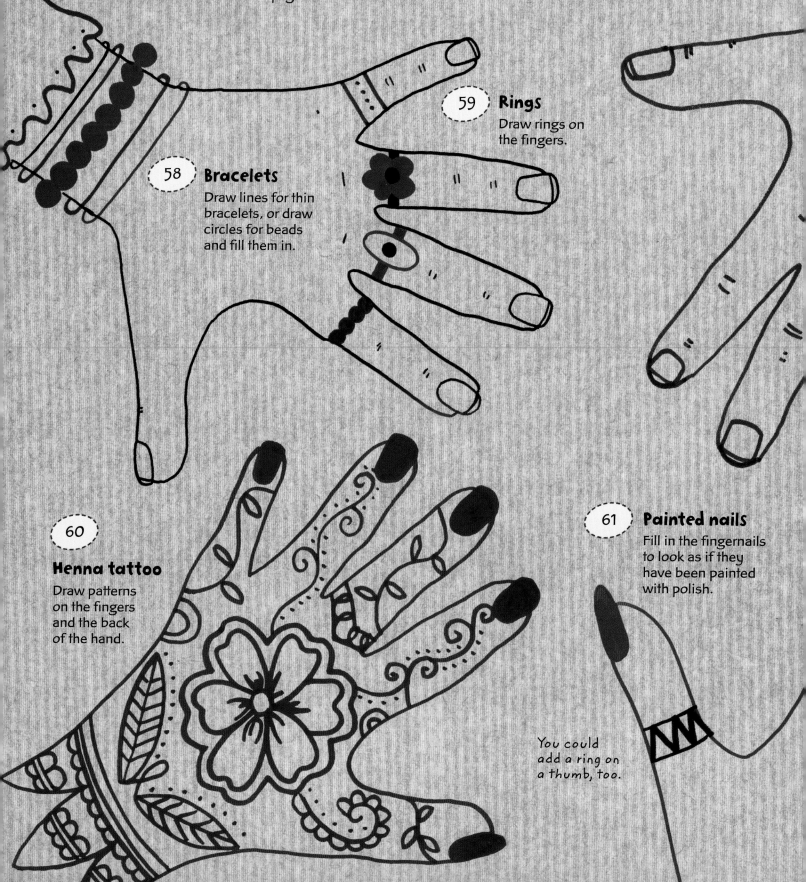

59 Rings
Draw rings on the fingers.

58 Bracelets
Draw lines for thin bracelets, or draw circles for beads and fill them in.

60

Henna tattoo
Draw patterns on the fingers and the back of the hand.

61 Painted nails
Fill in the fingernails to look as if they have been painted with polish.

You could add a ring on a thumb, too.

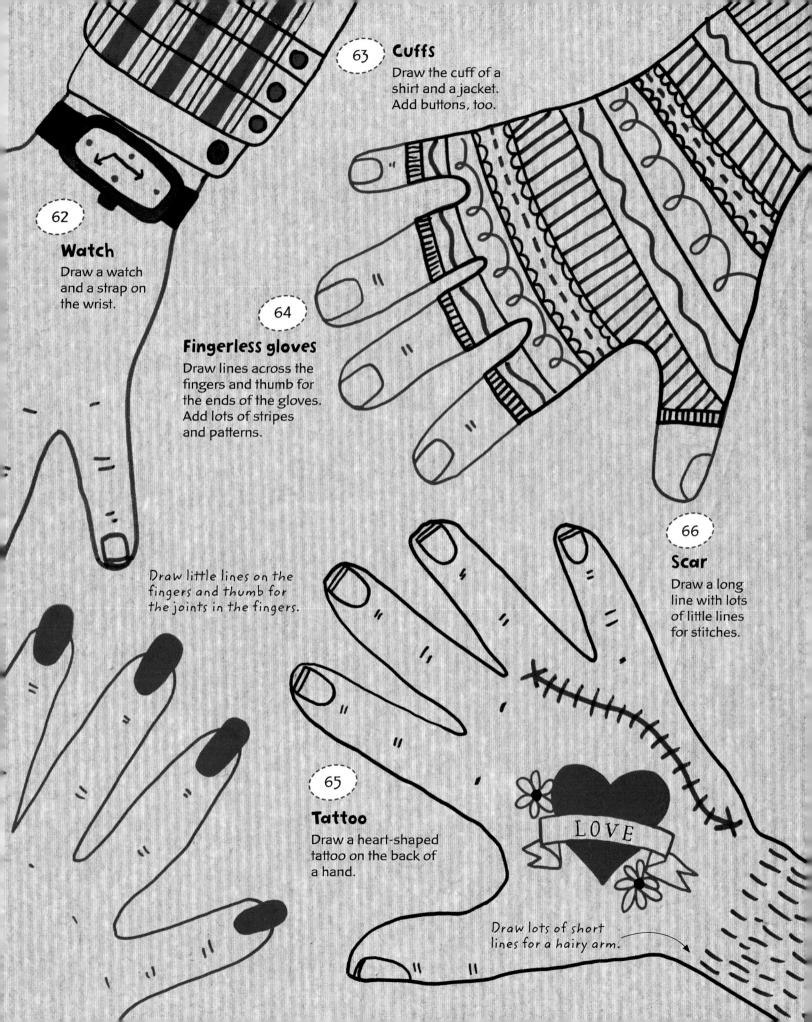

63 Cuffs

Draw the cuff of a shirt and a jacket. Add buttons, too.

62 Watch

Draw a watch and a strap on the wrist.

64 Fingerless gloves

Draw lines across the fingers and thumb for the ends of the gloves. Add lots of stripes and patterns.

Draw little lines on the fingers and thumb for the joints in the fingers.

66 Scar

Draw a long line with lots of little lines for stitches.

65 Tattoo

Draw a heart-shaped tattoo on the back of a hand.

LOVE

Draw lots of short lines for a hairy arm.

Futuristic cityscape

67 Copy the buildings on these pages to create a futuristic city, or use the ideas to design a city of your own.

68

Tall towers
Add different shapes of towers with satellite dishes or radio masts on top.

69 **Roads**
Draw lots of roads going between the buildings.

Cars and trucks
70 Draw lots of little cars and trucks to make the city look enormous.

You could add futuristic cars and buses flying through the sky.

71 Billboards

Draw large billboards with advertisements on the roofs of the buildings.

72 Windows

Draw individual windows in rows, or do lots of straight lines with a thick pen.

City cats

Use the ideas on these pages to draw a scene with cats on a street. Draw the shapes with a pencil, then fill them in with chalk pastels or chalks.

You could draw silhouettes of buildings in the background.

73 **Draw a cat**

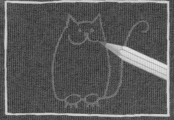 

1. Use a pencil to draw the outline of a cat. Draw its paws and a curly tail. Then, add the eyes, nose and mouth.

2. Draw lots of lines with chalk pastels across the body, and on the tail. Add thin whiskers. Then, draw over the outlines again.

Use a black pencil.

74

Sleeping cat

Draw a cat's body with one paw hanging down. Then, draw 'V' shapes on its side, for the eyes of a sleeping cat.

75

Wall

Draw a pencil line across the paper. Add the cats, then erase any lines inside their bodies.

76 Street light
Draw a lamppost and
fill it in with chalks.
Add a yellow lamp, and
yellow highlights along
one side of the post.

*Smudge
some chalk
for the glow
of the lamp.*

*You could
draw some
bricks on
the wall.*

78 Singing cat
Draw a cat with
its eyes shut
and an oval for
its mouth.

77 Cat and kittens
Draw a large cat.
Then, add a row of
little kittens behind it.

27

Crocodile pool

79 **Wax resist snake**

1. Draw four overlapping ovals for the coils of a snake. Draw a branch, then add the head and tail.

2. Draw patterns on the body with a white wax crayon (shown here in yellow). Then, fill in the snake with watery paint.

80 **Pool scene**

Draw a line for the edge of the pool across your paper. Add a tree, branches and some rocks. Fill them in with paints.

81 **Crocodile**

Draw a crocodile's head, eyes and body. Add markings with a white wax crayon, then paint over the top.

82 **Ripples**

Draw curved lines in the pool for ripples in the water. Brush blue paint on top.

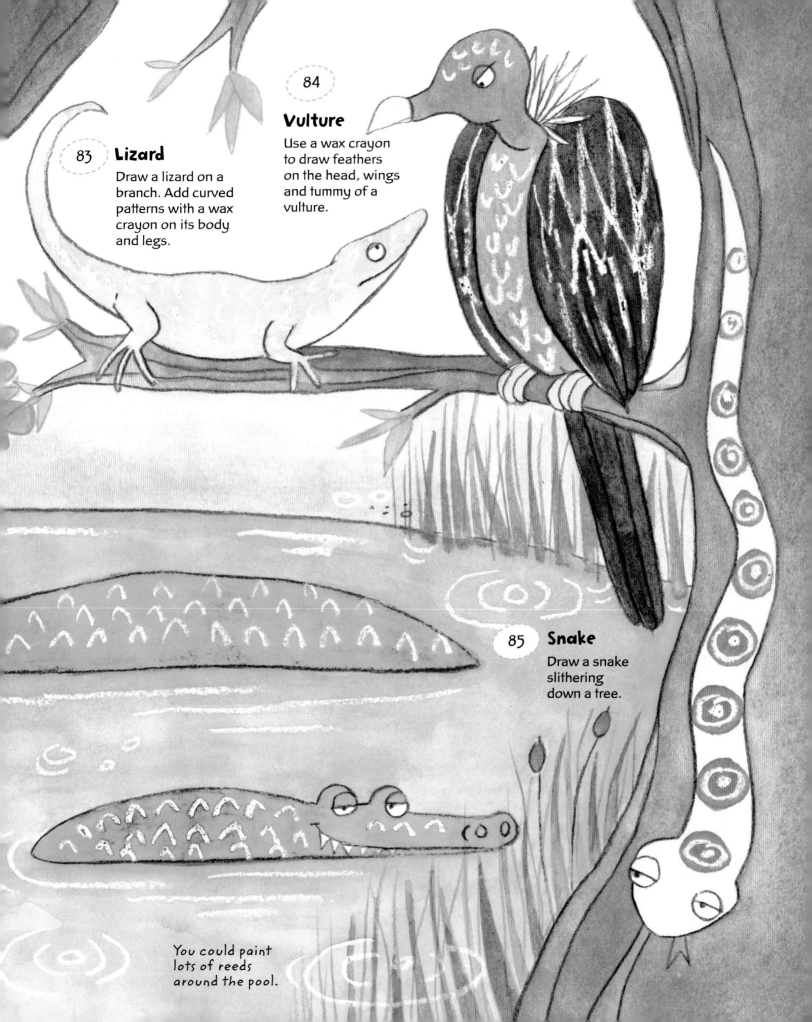

83 **Lizard**

Draw a lizard on a
branch. Add curved
patterns with a wax
crayon on its body
and legs.

84

Vulture

Use a wax crayon
to draw feathers
on the head, wings
and tummy of a
vulture.

85 **Snake**

Draw a snake
slithering
down a tree.

*You could paint
lots of reeds
around the pool.*

Take a line for a walk

Try drawing a picture, without lifting your pen off the paper. It's not easy, so you might need to cheat a little.

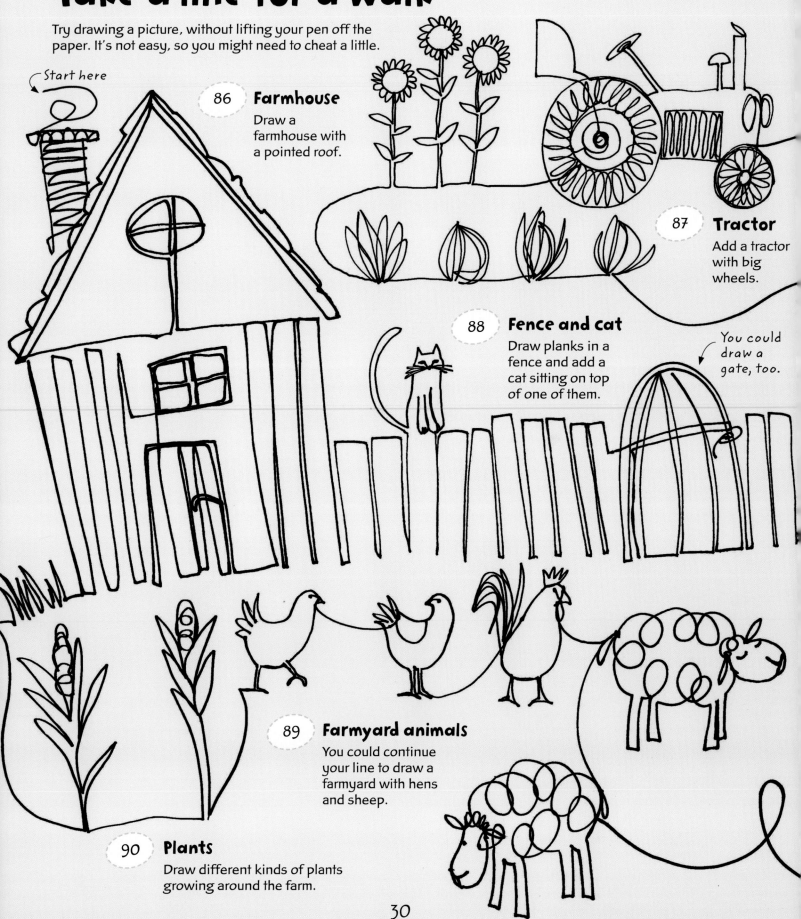

Start here

86 Farmhouse
Draw a farmhouse with a pointed roof.

87 Tractor
Add a tractor with big wheels.

88 Fence and cat
Draw planks in a fence and add a cat sitting on top of one of them.

You could draw a gate, too.

89 Farmyard animals
You could continue your line to draw a farmyard with hens and sheep.

90 Plants
Draw different kinds of plants growing around the farm.

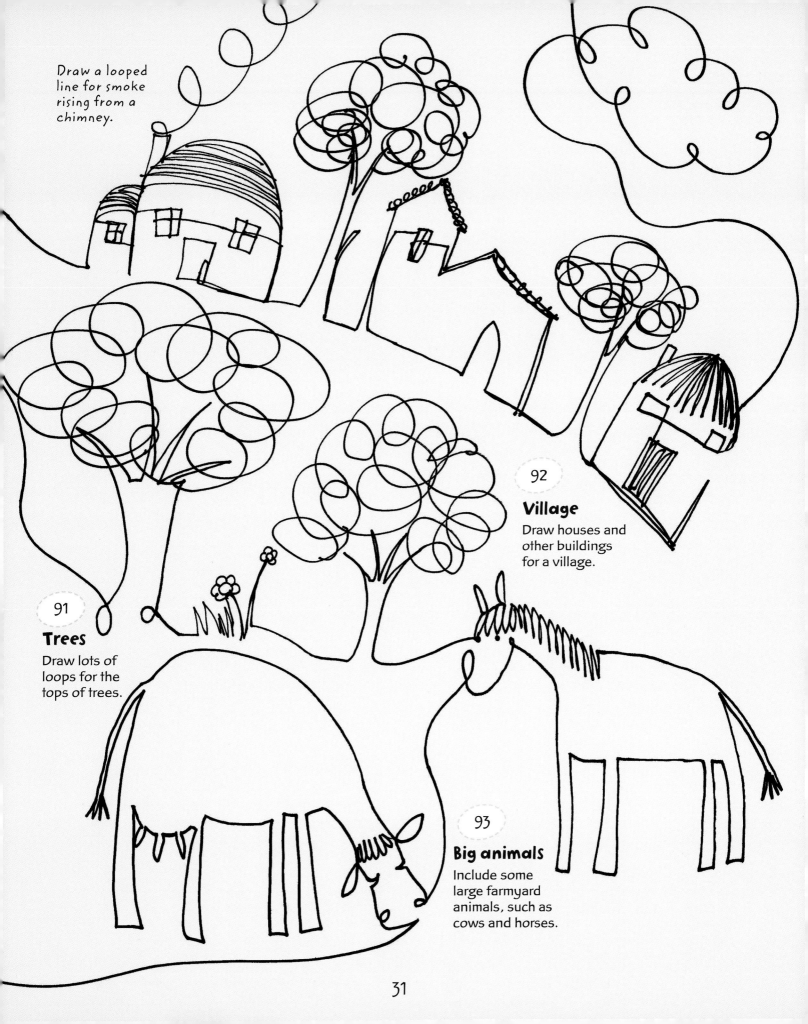

Draw a looped line for smoke rising from a chimney.

92

Village
Draw houses and other buildings for a village.

91

Trees
Draw lots of loops for the tops of trees.

93

Big animals
Include some large farmyard animals, such as cows and horses.

31

3-D street

95
Washing line
Glue on two strips of cardboard for posts. Add string for the line and paper clothes.

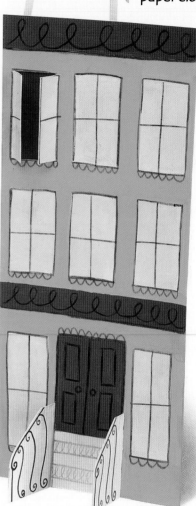

You could slot two pieces of cardboard onto a house, as railings.

94 **Make a house**

Make the front door the height of the strip.

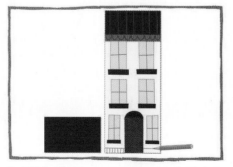

Open the door to make the house stand up.

1. Cut a long, narrow piece of thin cardboard. Then, cut a strip off the bottom for the front door. Draw a roof, and windows with window sills. Add a doorway, too.

2. Fill in the house with paint. Paint the strip for the door on both sides. When the paint is dry, use pencils to draw window frames, tiles on the roof and railings.

3. Cut along the left-hand side of the doorway. Then, slot the door into the cut and fold the strip over on the back to secure the door. Draw details on the door.

96 **Roof garden**

Cut out pots and plants from cardboard and glue them onto the roof.

97

Your home

Make a model of your home in the same way, or design a house that you would like to live in.

98

Double doors

Make two doors that meet in the middle when they are closed.

You could draw a flower in a pot in an open window.

Chalky fish picture

99 **Fish**

1. Use a chalk pastel or chalk to draw a fish's body, tail and fins. Then, smudge the shapes a little with a fingertip.

2. Using a pencil, draw around the body, fins and tail. Add lines to them, too. Draw an eye and mouth, and spots on the body.

3. Draw a circle around some of the spots with a pale pastel. Then, draw around the pastel circles with the pencil.

100 **Sea**

Draw long wavy lines for the surface of the sea. Smudge them with your fingertip, then draw pencil lines on top.

101 **Jellyfish**

Use a white chalk pastel to draw a jellyfish and its tentacles. Draw the outlines with a pencil.

You could draw a fish with a long wavy tail.

102

Seaweed

Draw seaweed with different shades of green chalk pastels and pencils.

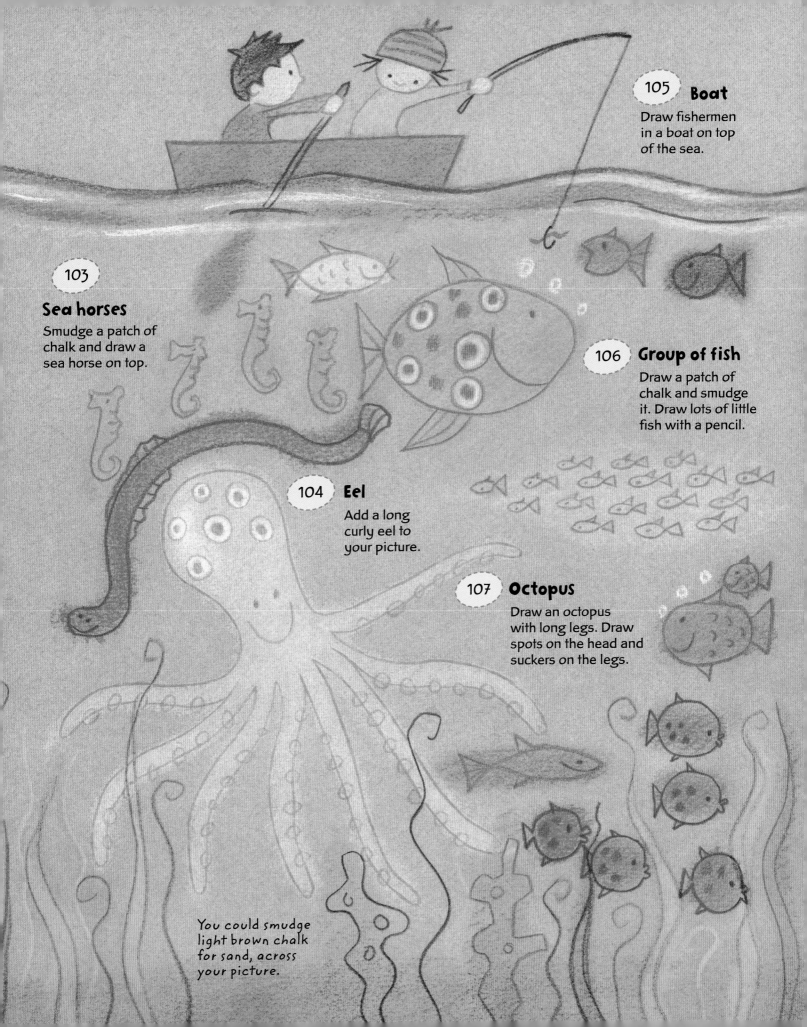

105 Boat
Draw fishermen in a boat on top of the sea.

103

Sea horses
Smudge a patch of chalk and draw a sea horse on top.

106 Group of fish
Draw a patch of chalk and smudge it. Draw lots of little fish with a pencil.

104 Eel
Add a long curly eel to your picture.

107 Octopus
Draw an octopus with long legs. Draw spots on the head and suckers on the legs.

You could smudge light brown chalk for sand, across your picture.

Sporty drawings

Copy the ideas on these pages to draw sporty people in different poses. Use a thin black pen and pencils.

108 **Kicking and heading**
Draw someone heading a ball or kicking a ball behind them.

109 **Bright clothes**
Fill in parts of a player's shirt and shorts with bright pencils.

Draw lines beside the figures and balls to make them look as if they are moving.

110 **Goalie**
Draw a goalkeeper wearing gloves diving for a ball.

111 **Match play**
Draw two players from different teams playing against each other in a match.

Draw a circle with curved lines for a basketball.

113

Shooting
Include a tall player about to shoot at the basket.

112

Bouncing ball
Draw a player bouncing a ball along the ground.

114 **Markings**
Draw numbers on the players' shirts, and stripes on their shirts and shorts.

Perching birds

115 Bird on a wire

Use a thick paintbrush.

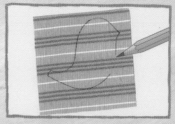

1. Mix lots of watery blue paint. Brush it all over a piece of thick paper, then leave it to dry.

2. Use a pencil to draw a line across the paper for a telephone wire that the bird will perch on.

3. Draw the outline of a bird on a piece of material. Then, cut it out and glue it on just above the wire.

4. Use a ballpoint pen to draw a curved line on its body. Then, add an eye, a beak, a wing and legs.

116 Make a picture

Paint a large piece of paper and draw several telephone wires across it. Add lots of birds.

You could glue a shape onto a bird's head, then draw an eye on top.

117 Branches

Cut branches from paper and glue them on. Add leaves cut from different scraps of material.

118 Nest and eggs

Scribble lines with a ballpoint pen for a nest. Glue on eggs cut from pieces of material.

Add a little
bird flying
in the sky.

119 Fancy tail
Cut some feathers from
scraps of material and
glue them onto the tail.

120 Clouds
Cut wavy shapes
from pieces of
material. Glue them
on, then add lots
of spiral patterns.

You could draw
patterns on the
tail feathers.

Try drawing extra
feathers on the
birds' tummies.

121 Little bird
Make birds of
different sizes
perching on
the wires.

You could cut a
wing from a piece
of material, too.

Lots of pipes

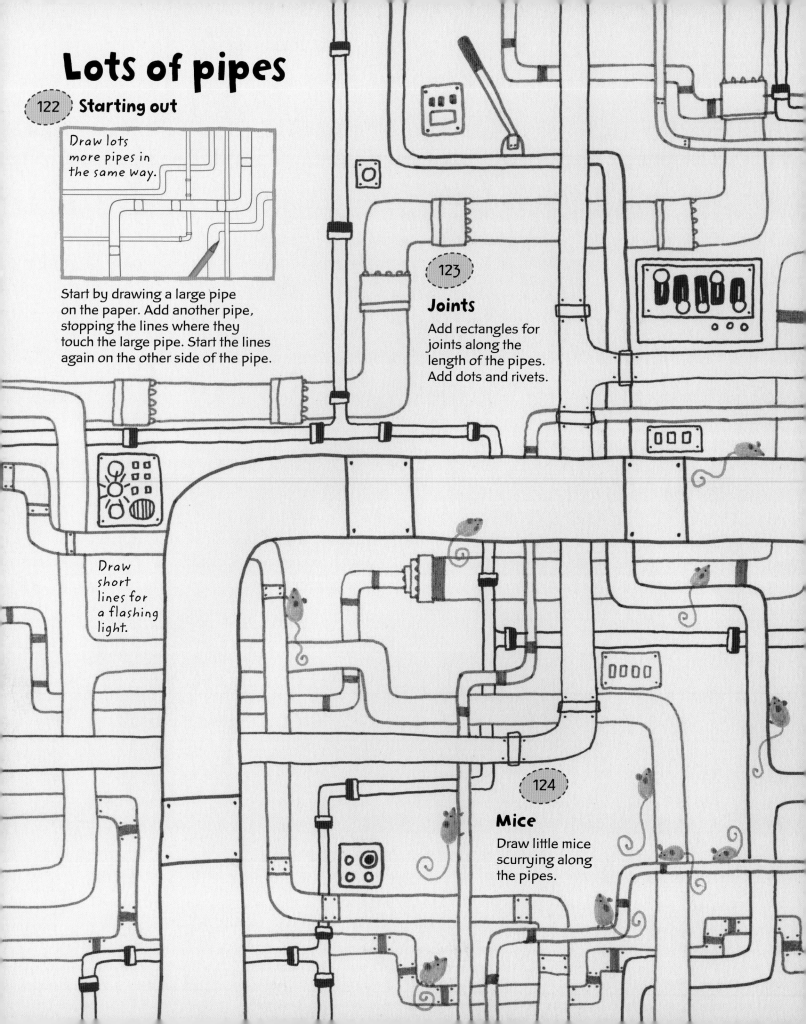

122 Starting out

Draw lots more pipes in the same way.

Start by drawing a large pipe on the paper. Add another pipe, stopping the lines where they touch the large pipe. Start the lines again on the other side of the pipe.

Draw short lines for a flashing light.

123 Joints

Add rectangles for joints along the length of the pipes. Add dots and rivets.

124 Mice

Draw little mice scurrying along the pipes.

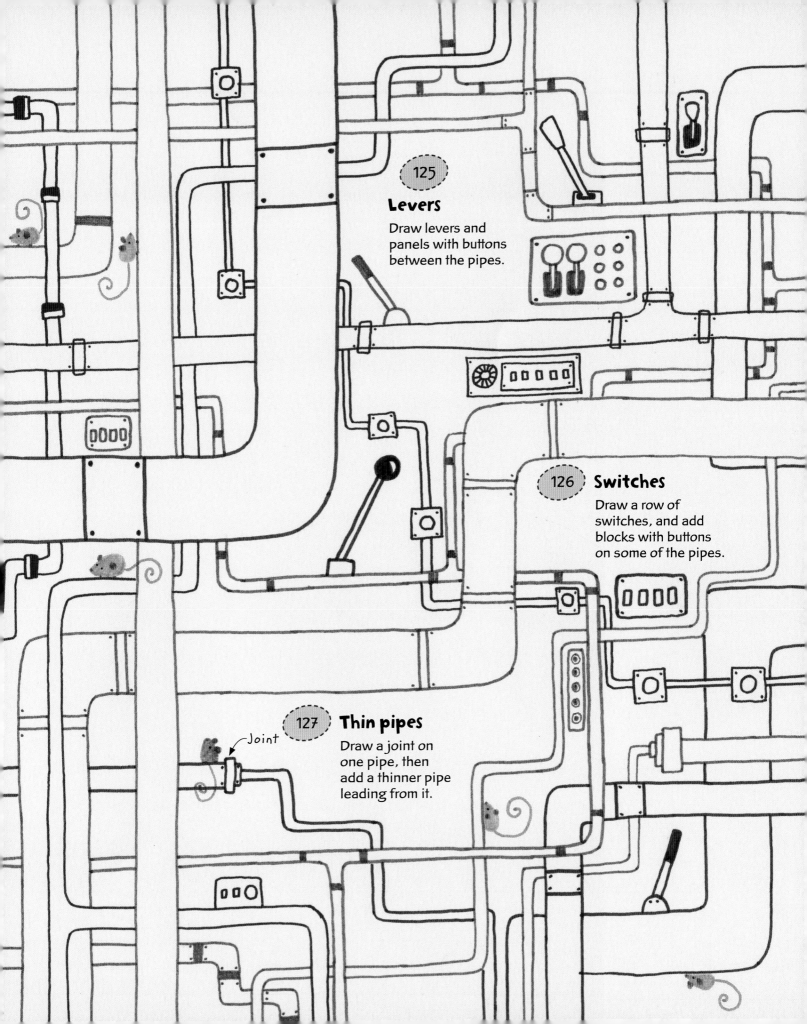

125
Levers
Draw levers and panels with buttons between the pipes.

126 Switches
Draw a row of switches, and add blocks with buttons on some of the pipes.

Joint

127 Thin pipes
Draw a joint on one pipe, then add a thinner pipe leading from it.

Reindeer decorations

128 **Reindeer**

Tape the antlers on the back of the head.

1. Draw the outline of a reindeer on a piece of thin cardboard and cut it out. Then, cut two long, thin strips from cardboard. These are for the antlers.

2. Paint the reindeer with thick, red paint. Quickly, before the paint dries, use a toothpick to scratch patterns in the paint. Paint the strips and scratch a line along them.

3. Cut one of the strips in half, then cut the remaining strip into smaller pieces. Glue the short pieces onto the longer ones to make two antlers. Tape them onto the head.

All the white shapes on these pages were made from red cardboard, painted with white paint.

129 **Reindeer chain**

Make several reindeer and tape them onto a ribbon or a piece of string.

42

130 Stars

Cut out stars and decorate them. If you are going to hang them on a tree or in a window, glue on another star, back to back.

You could tape gift ribbon to the back of a heart or star.

131 Hanging hearts

Make several hearts and use ribbon to hang them up.

Painting trees

All the trees on these pages were painted with a brush and black ink. Some have details added with white paint or a black felt-tip pen.

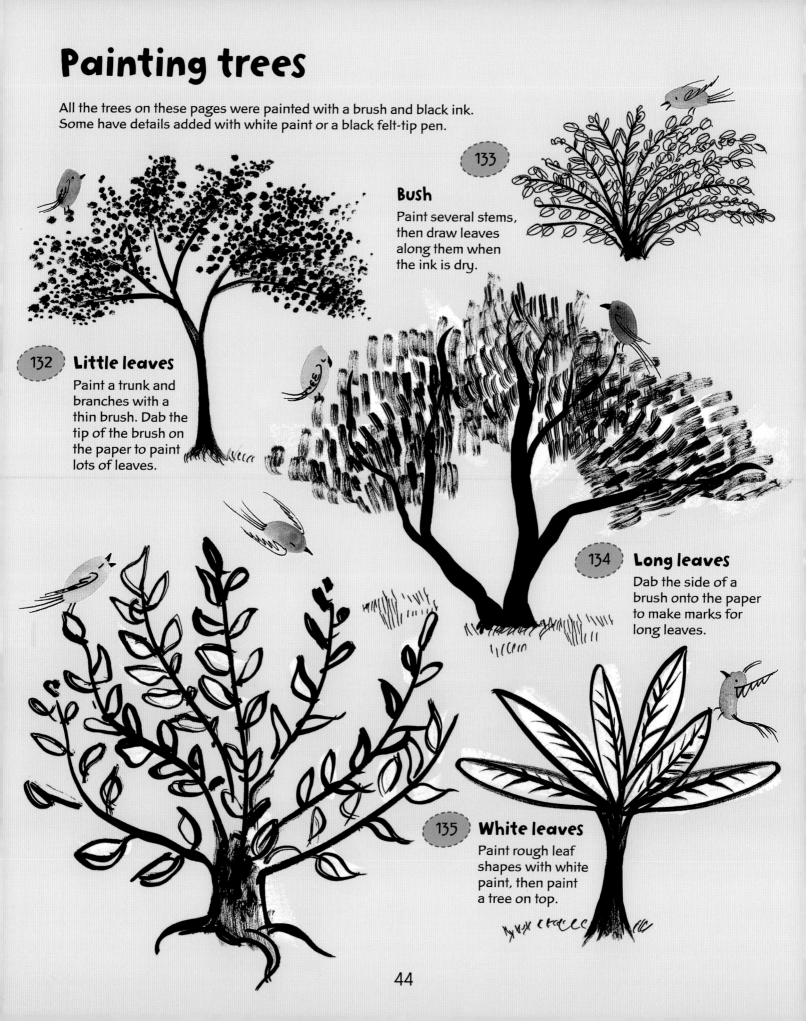

133

Bush
Paint several stems, then draw leaves along them when the ink is dry.

132 **Little leaves**
Paint a trunk and branches with a thin brush. Dab the tip of the brush on the paper to paint lots of leaves.

134 **Long leaves**
Dab the side of a brush onto the paper to make marks for long leaves.

135 **White leaves**
Paint rough leaf shapes with white paint, then paint a tree on top.

136 Curly leaves

Paint the trunk and branches of a tree. Then, use a pen to draw around and around for groups of leaves.

137 Birds

Fingerprint bright birds around the trees. Draw their beaks, wings and tails with a felt-tip pen.

You could print a bird, then draw its wings stretched out, like this.

138 Grass

Draw blades of grass around the bottom of a tree with a felt-tip pen.

For leaves like these, dab the bristles of a big brush onto the paper again and again.

Out in space

139 Rocket

Draw a circle in each window.

1. Draw the outline of a rocket on white paper. Cut it out and glue it onto another piece of paper.

2. Cut out three windows and glue them on. Cut strips of red and blue paper and glue them on.

140 Stars

Draw different sizes of stars with a white pencil.

3. Draw fins with a white pencil and add lines across them. Draw orange and yellow flames, too.

142 Planets

Use pencils to draw planets. Add some circular craters, too.

141

Striped rocket

Draw stripes across a rocket and fill them in. Glue fins and windows on top.

143 Ringed planet
Draw a planet, then cut out a 'ring' from paper and glue it on top.

144 Large planet
Draw a large planet bleeding off the corner of the paper.

145 Flying saucer
Cut the top and bottom parts of a flying saucer from paper. Then, draw its rocket boosters and add dots for windows.

Hungry rats

146 **Draw a rat**

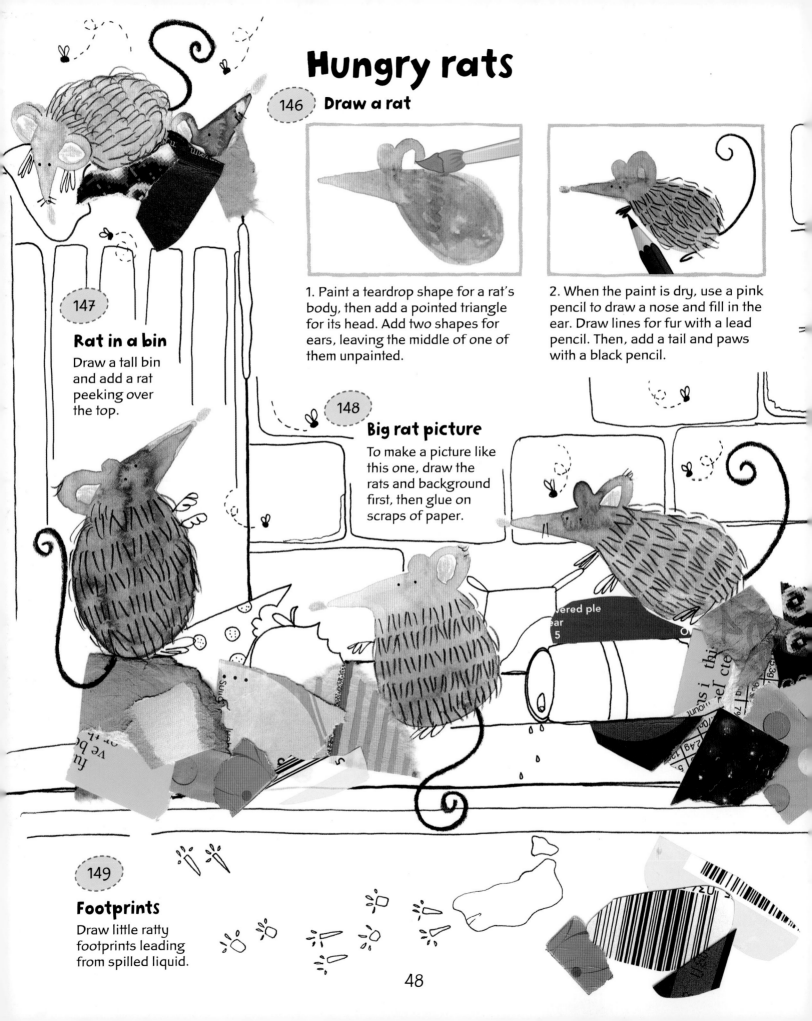

1. Paint a teardrop shape for a rat's body, then add a pointed triangle for its head. Add two shapes for ears, leaving the middle of one of them unpainted.

2. When the paint is dry, use a pink pencil to draw a nose and fill in the ear. Draw lines for fur with a lead pencil. Then, add a tail and paws with a black pencil.

147

Rat in a bin

Draw a tall bin and add a rat peeking over the top.

148

Big rat picture

To make a picture like this one, draw the rats and background first, then glue on scraps of paper.

149

Footprints

Draw little ratty footprints leading from spilled liquid.

Add a snail.

150

Drainpipe

Draw a drainpipe, and add brackets and screws fixing it to a wall.

151

Climbing rat

Paint a rat overlapping a drainpipe, like this.

152

Smelly rat

Use a thin pen to draw flies buzzing around a rat's head.

You could add a spider and its web.

153

Shy rat

Glue scraps of paper on first, then paint a rat's head and ears.

Use scraps of paper from magazines and packaging in your recycling bin.

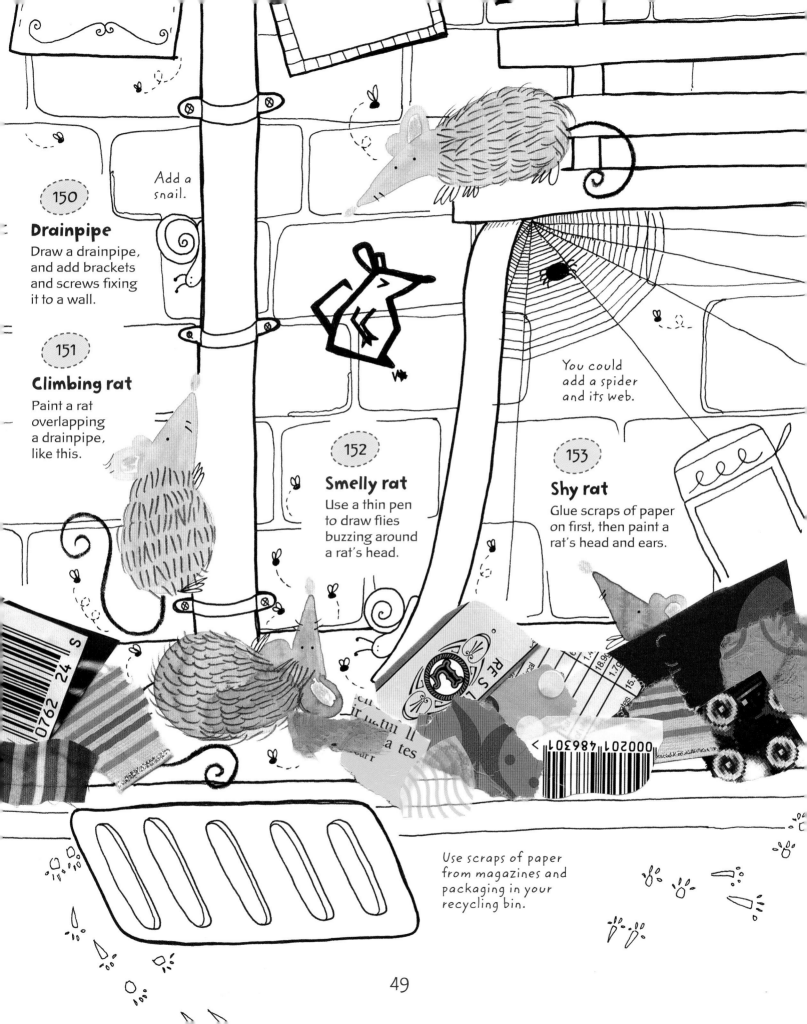

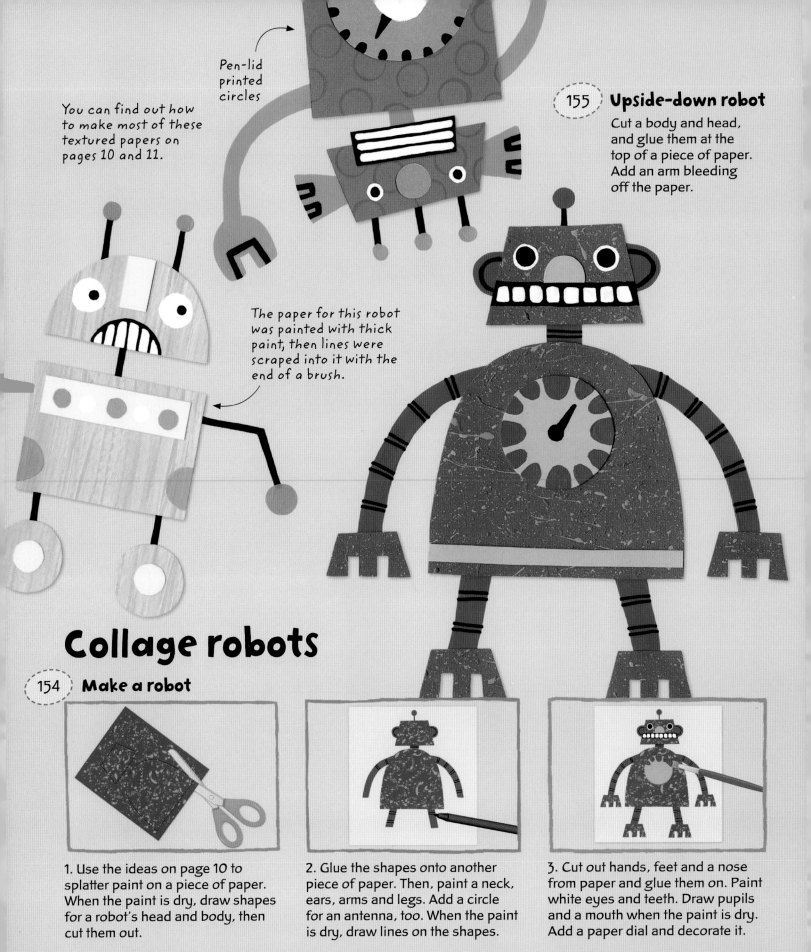

Pen-lid printed circles

You can find out how to make most of these textured papers on pages 10 and 11.

155 **Upside-down robot**
Cut a body and head, and glue them at the top of a piece of paper. Add an arm bleeding off the paper.

The paper for this robot was painted with thick paint, then lines were scraped into it with the end of a brush.

Collage robots

154 **Make a robot**

1. Use the ideas on page 10 to splatter paint on a piece of paper. When the paint is dry, draw shapes for a robot's head and body, then cut them out.

2. Glue the shapes onto another piece of paper. Then, paint a neck, ears, arms and legs. Add a circle for an antenna, too. When the paint is dry, draw lines on the shapes.

3. Cut out hands, feet and a nose from paper and glue them on. Paint white eyes and teeth. Draw pupils and a mouth when the paint is dry. Add a paper dial and decorate it.

157 **Robot pet**
Make a robot pet.
Glue the head onto the
body. Paint ears and
feet, and add a tail.

Stippled
paper

Finger-printed
spots

156 **Geometric robot**
Make a robot with
a rectangular head.
Cut a triangle for
the body, then cut
off the pointed end.

This paper was
printed with
bubble wrap.

This robot's head
and body were
dry-brushed.

You could make a
robot with chunky
hands and feet.

Simple faces

158 Basic head shapes

Draw these head shapes and necks. Then, try to draw the shape of your own head.

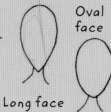
Long face

Oval face

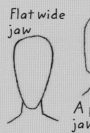
Head at an angle

Flat wide jaw

A pointed jaw

159 Simple faces

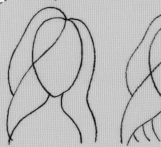

1. Draw an oval head. Add a neck and shoulders. Then, draw wavy lines for hair, and add some clothes.

2. Add eyes, eyebrows, a nose and mouth. Then, draw lots of wavy lines in the hair.

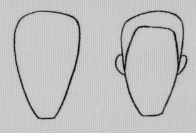

1. Draw a wide head with a flat chin. Then, draw the hairline and add ears about halfway down the head.

2. Add eyes, eyebrows, a nose and mouth. Then, add a neck and shoulders. Draw lines in the hair.

160 Side-on head (profile)

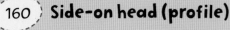
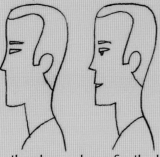

Copy the shape above for the head and shoulders. Add the hairline, an eyebrow, eye and mouth.

Draw an oval face with a small nose and pointed chin. Add wavy hair, an eye, eyebrow and lips.

161 Noses and eyebrows

Draw a head, then add a nose and eyebrows.

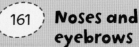
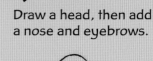

162 Eyes

Add eyes to a face.

Looking sideways

163 Mouths

Try different types of mouths.

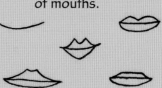

1. Draw four different head shapes, necks and shoulders, leaving a small space between each person.

2. Fill the spaces between the heads with lots of hair. Then, draw more lines in each person's hair.

3. Draw over the lines with a ballpoint pen. Then, fill everything in with watery paints.

Bug collection

165 Making a bug

Use a black felt-tip pen.

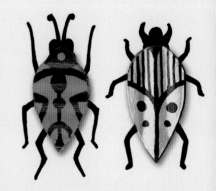

1. Draw the shape of a bug's body on a scrap of corrugated cardboard. Cut it out, then paint it.

2. When the paint is dry, glue the body onto a piece of paper. Then, draw the head, legs and feelers.

3. Draw curved lines across the top of the body, and a line down the middle. Then, add patterns.

167

Spots

Make a spotted bug. Look at the patterns on the bugs in this row for ideas.

You could make lots of different bugs and glue them onto some paper in rows.

166

Bug bodies

Make different bugs by changing the shapes of their bodies.

168

Shaded bugs

Paint part of a bug's body with one shade of paint, then blend another shade into it.

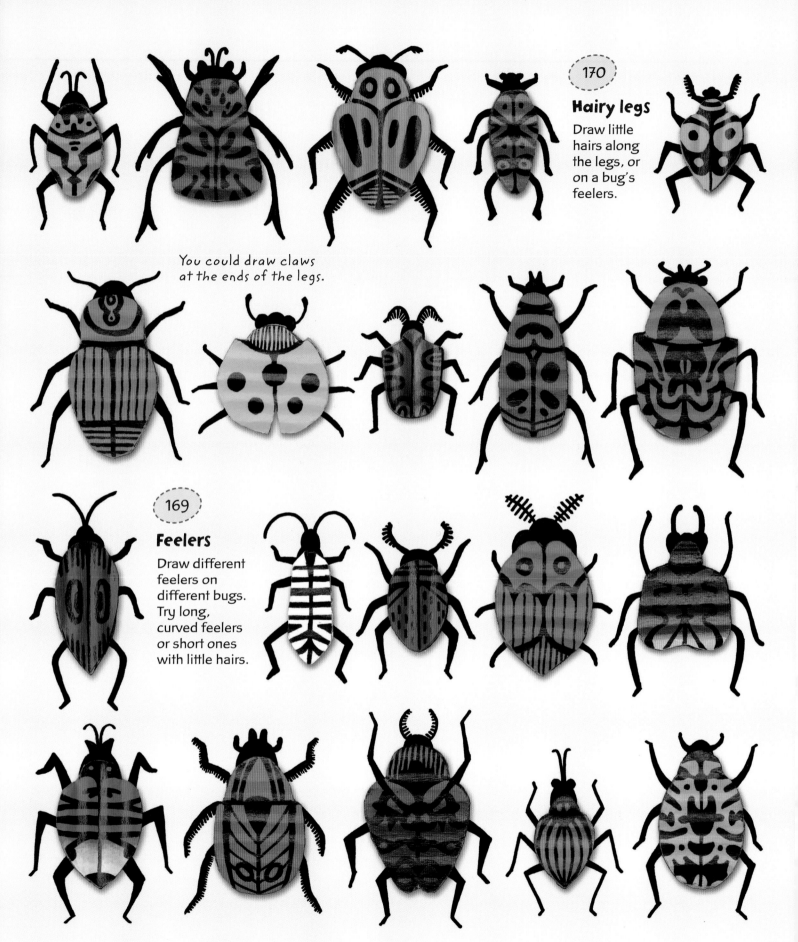

170

Hairy legs

Draw little hairs along the legs, or on a bug's feelers.

You could draw claws at the ends of the legs.

169

Feelers

Draw different feelers on different bugs. Try long, curved feelers or short ones with little hairs.

Spooky castle

171 **Castle**

1. Draw lines for the rocks at the bottom of your paper. Add castle walls, towers and roofs.

2. Go over the lines with a felt-tip pen, making them slightly wobbly. Add a door, windows, rocks and steps.

3. Paint over the castle with watery black paint. Don't worry if the pen lines bleed into it.

4. Add some patches of watery purple paint. Then, fill in the sky with very watery paint.

You could draw some scribbly trees and bushes.

172 **Cloud and mountains**

Draw a cloud behind the castle, and some mountains beside it. Fill them in with watery paints.

173 **Bats**

Draw some bats flying around the castle. Fill them in with watery black paint.

Night animals

Use the ideas shown on these pages to print and paint a scene with night animals.

174   **Tree**

Drag the paint to make thicker lines.

Dip the edge of a piece of cardboard into thick white paint, then print a trunk and branches on a piece of blue paper.

175   **Bat**

1. Fingerprint a body. Then, paint the wings and let them dry. Draw lines on the wings with chalk.

2. Print yellow eyes with the end of a paintbrush. Draw dots in the eyes, then add feet and ears.

You could paint a snowy hill at the bottom of your picture.

177 Owls

Fingerprint a body, and use the end of a paintbrush to print the eyes. Then, draw a beak and add patterns for feathers.

176 Fox

Twist the cardboard to print a triangle.

1. Dip the edge of a piece of cardboard into orange paint. Then, print a triangular head.

Draw around the tail, too.

2. Fingerpaint a body and tail. Then, print the legs with cardboard. Draw ears, eyes and a nose when the paint is dry.

178 Snowflakes

Use the end of a paintbrush to print lots of snowflakes in the sky.

These paw prints were printed with the corner of a piece of cardboard.

Crazy doodles

179 **Star doodle**

Draw several stars, leaving spaces between them. Then, doodle some lines to join the shapes.

You could fill in some parts of your doodle with pencils.

180 **Planets**

Doodle some planets between the stars. Join them together with straight and wavy lines.

182 **Boat**

Doodle a boat on the wavy lines.

Fish and seaweed

181 Start by drawing the fish and some seaweed. Then, fill the spaces with wavy lines.

60

183 **Birds**

Doodle lots of birds flying around. Join them with wavy lines.

184 **Cats**

Draw cats in different positions and fill the spaces with lines.

Draw a cat asleep on a mat.

Tropical birds

185 Simple bird

1. Paint a shape for the bird's body with thick paint. Then, paint several lines for tail feathers.

2. When the paint is dry, paint a beak. Add thin lines for legs. Then, paint an eye and a wing.

186 Big bird

1. Paint a large, curved body, with looping shapes for the tail. Leave the paint to dry.

Paint head feathers, too.

2. Paint a bright orange beak. Then, paint the legs, a wing and dots on the tail. Add an eye.

187 Flowers

Paint flowers with bright paints. When dry, add more circles of paint in the middles.

189 **Flying bird**

Paint a curved body. Then, add a wing stretching out on either side of the body.

188 **Tropical leaves**

Paint a thin line for a stalk. Then, paint leaves along both sides of the stalk.

You could paint some berries among the leaves.

Pen and ink drawings

All the pictures on these pages were drawn with an ink pen (fountain pen or dip pen) and filled in with paint, pens or pencils. If you don't have an ink pen use a black felt-tip pen instead.

190 **Hats and bags**

Draw a selection of hats and bags. Fill them in completely or add patterns to them.

You could draw a spotted sun hat.

This red bag was drawn with a pencil first, then the pen detail was added.

Add a button to a bag.

191 **Shoes**

Draw different styles of shoes. You could draw them from overhead or as a side view.

You could draw a bag with a short handle, or a long strap.

193

Cakes on plates
Draw the cake first,
then add the plate
around it.

192 Sundaes

Draw a glass,
then fill it with
an ice-cream
sundae.

You could draw
lots of stripes
for a straw.

Paint several
stripes for the
layers in a cake.

Cupcake party

194 **Paint a cupcake**

1. Paint a shape for a cupcake using pale brown paint. Let it dry. Use a thin brush to paint a face near the top of the cake.

2. Use thick paint to paint a paper case at the bottom of the cupcake. Then, scratch lines into the wet paint with the end of a brush.

The paint may take a while to dry.

3. Mix thick paint with white glue in an old container. Then, spread the paint over the top of the cupcake. Let it dry.

195 **Cake stand**
Use a pencil to draw a cake stand beneath some cupcakes, then fill it in with paint.

This shadow was added with a blue pencil.

196

Toppings

Use the ideas shown on these two pages to decorate the top of the cupcakes. Draw the shapes on paper, cut them out and glue them on.

Pencil lines for strings

197

Balloons

Paint a little arm and hand, and some balloons.

Use dark brown paint for a chocolate cupcake.

198 ### Sugar sprinkles

Sprinkle glitter onto the wet paint. Shake off any excess glitter when the paint is dry.

Deep-sea fish

Draw a deep-sea scene with chalks or chalk pastels on a piece of black paper.

199 Simple fish

1. Draw an oval with a chalk pastel or chalk. Then, run your finger along it to smudge it.

2. Draw two shapes for the tail. Then, use a pencil to draw a fin on either side of the body.

3. Paint a little white circle for the eye. When the paint is dry, draw a black dot in the middle of it.

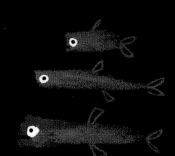

201 Group of fish
Draw lots of identical fish swimming together.

200

Long eels
Draw a long wiggly shape for an eel's body. Smudge the end of the tail. Draw fins and teeth with a pencil.

202

Big teeth
Cut a little strip of cardboard and use it to print a row of sharp teeth.

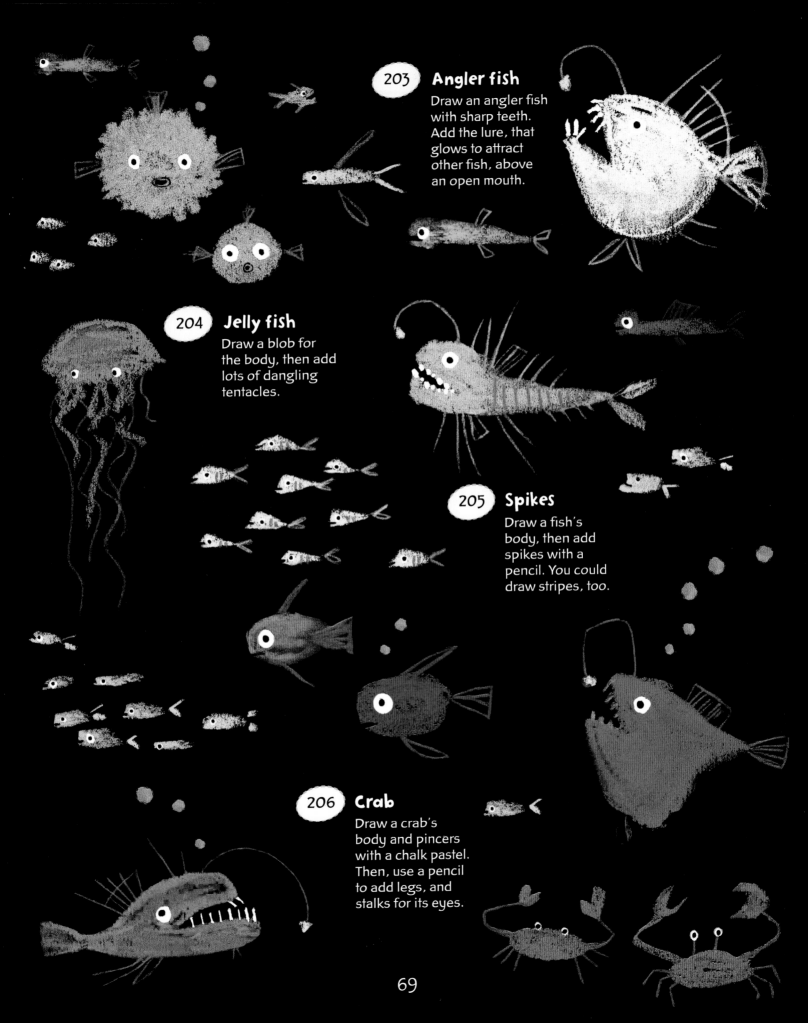

203 Angler fish

Draw an angler fish with sharp teeth. Add the lure, that glows to attract other fish, above an open mouth.

204 Jelly fish

Draw a blob for the body, then add lots of dangling tentacles.

205 Spikes

Draw a fish's body, then add spikes with a pencil. You could draw stripes, too.

206 Crab

Draw a crab's body and pincers with a chalk pastel. Then, use a pencil to add legs, and stalks for its eyes.

Fruit and flower patterns

207 Strawberries and daisies

Leave spaces between the shapes.

1. Paint some bright red strawberry shapes on a piece of paper. Let them dry. Then, paint some yellow circles between them for the middles of the daisies.

2. Paint green leaves between the shapes. Then, dip the tip of a paintbrush into black paint and dab it several times onto each strawberry, for seeds. Let them dry.

3. Use pencils to draw a stalk on each strawberry. Then, draw petals around each daisy. Use a green pencil to draw around the leaves. Then, add lots of curling stalks.

208 Flowers

Decorate a piece of paper with flowers. Paint purple, red and yellow circles for the middles of the flowers, and green shapes for leaves.

209 Leaves

Paint orange, green and brown leaves. Draw jagged lines around them but don't worry if you go over the edge of the painted shapes.

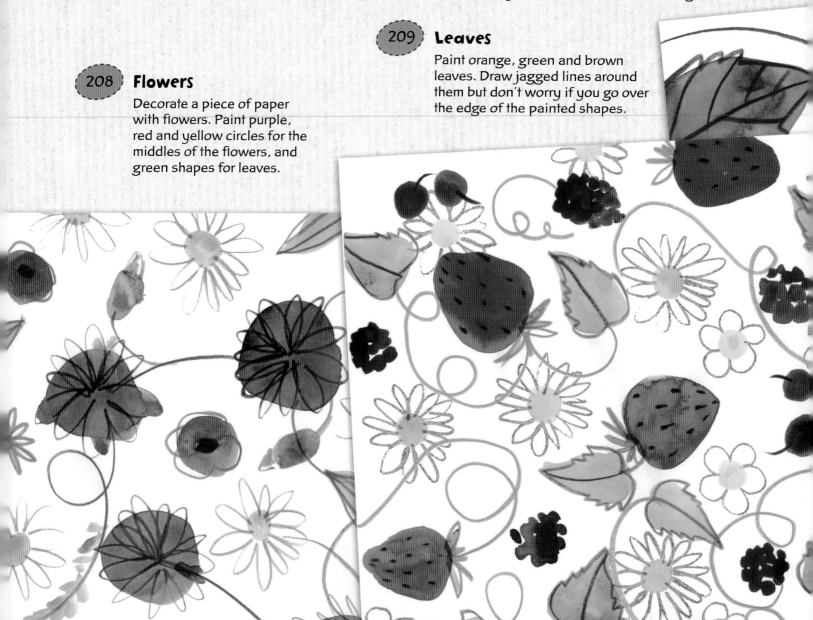

210 **Vegetables**

Paint a pattern with vegetables. Add little flowers to fill the spaces between them.

Printed snakes

211 Simple snake

1. Draw a snake's head with an open mouth. Then, add the body and tail. Cut out the shape.

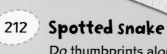

Lay the snake on newspaper.

2. Cut a triangle from a kitchen sponge and dip it into some paint. Print shapes along the body.

3. When the paint has dried, use a pen to draw eyes and nostrils. Then, glue on paper fangs.

212 Spotted snake

Do thumbprints along one side of the body. When the paint is dry do a fingerprinted shape on each print.

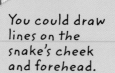

You could draw lines on the snake's cheek and forehead.

213 Stripes

Use the edge of two pieces of a kitchen sponge to print stripes along a snake.

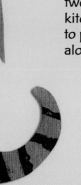

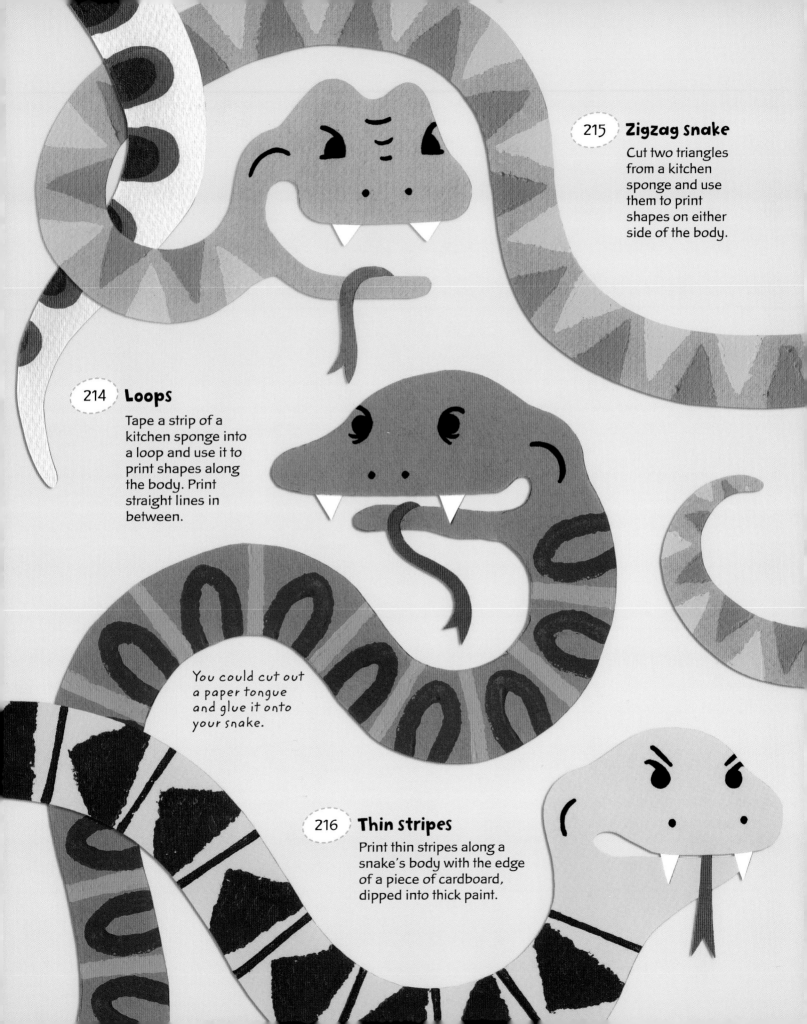

215 **Zigzag Snake**

Cut two triangles from a kitchen sponge and use them to print shapes on either side of the body.

214 **Loops**

Tape a strip of a kitchen sponge into a loop and use it to print shapes along the body. Print straight lines in between.

You could cut out a paper tongue and glue it onto your snake.

216 **Thin stripes**

Print thin stripes along a snake's body with the edge of a piece of cardboard, dipped into thick paint.

Day and night

This picture is drawn as one large scene. You then cut it in half so that you can paint one side in sunset shades, and the other side as night.

217 Making the scene

1. Draw wavy lines for hills and a valley across a piece of thick white paper. Add some lines for paths and roads, too.

2. Add people, buildings, trees and a bus. Draw long shadows, too. Then, add a sun on one side and moon on the other.

218 Sun

Use orange and yellow pencils to draw a glow around the sun. Fill it in with chalk.

You could draw lots of kites to fill the sky.

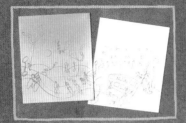

3. Cut the picture in half. Paint the left side all over with pale yellow paint. Add orange across the top while the paint is still wet.

4. Do the same to the other side with two shades of blue paint. When it's dry, fill in everything with darker shades of paint.

5. When all the paint is dry, tape the two sides together again. Try to match the shapes in the middle as well as you can.

6. Use pencils to add details to all the shapes. Add some darker shading on them. Then, use chalk to fill in the sun and moon.

Smudge the chalk around the edge of the moon.

219 **Lights**

Draw a glow from a streetlight and the beam from the bus's headlight with white chalk.

Laboratory experiments

220 Draw a scene

Use a pen or pencil to draw a rectangle for a workbench. Add flasks, bottles, a Bunsen burner and tripods. Then, use the ideas on these pages for adding paint.

221 Blow-painting

The paint should spread across the paper.

Blob some runny paint onto the paper. Hold a straw over the paint and blow hard. If the paint dries too quickly, blob on some more.

222 Bunsen burner

Blow-paint yellow and orange flames above the burner, then print some bubbling liquid.

The liquids in these flasks were painted with a brush, then blow-painted and printed shapes were added.

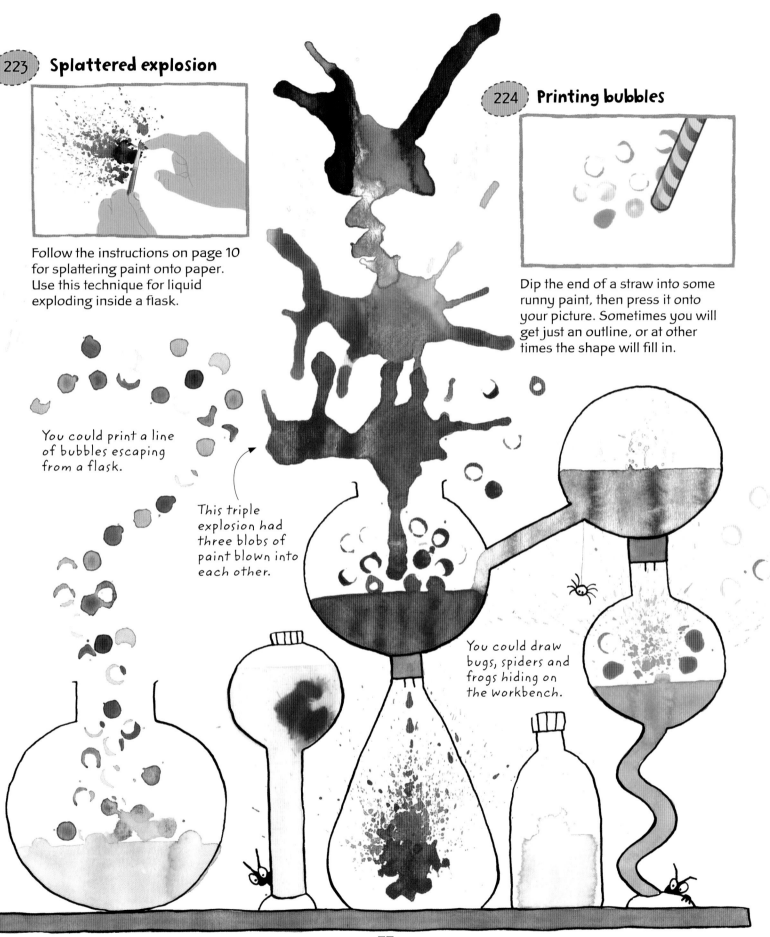

223 Splattered explosion

Follow the instructions on page 10 for splattering paint onto paper. Use this technique for liquid exploding inside a flask.

224 Printing bubbles

Dip the end of a straw into some runny paint, then press it onto your picture. Sometimes you will get just an outline, or at other times the shape will fill in.

You could print a line of bubbles escaping from a flask.

This triple explosion had three blobs of paint blown into each other.

You could draw bugs, spiders and frogs hiding on the workbench.

226 **Squirrel**

Draw a squirrel with a curly tail, perched on a branch.

227 **Bird**

Draw birds with curly head and tail feathers.

228

Trees

Paint thick stripes for tree trunks, then draw branches with ink.

Curly forest animals

All the curly lines on these two pages were drawn using a ink pen and brown ink.

225 **Deer**

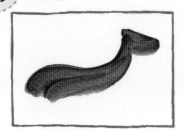

1. Mix brown paint with some water, then paint a wavy shape for a deer's body. Paint a head, too.

2. When the paint is dry, draw the outline of a deer's head and body with an ink pen or felt-tip pen.

3. Draw an eye, a nose, an ear and curly antlers on the head. Then, add spirals on the body.

4. Draw four legs with curly shapes at the ends for the hooves. Then, add a curly tail.

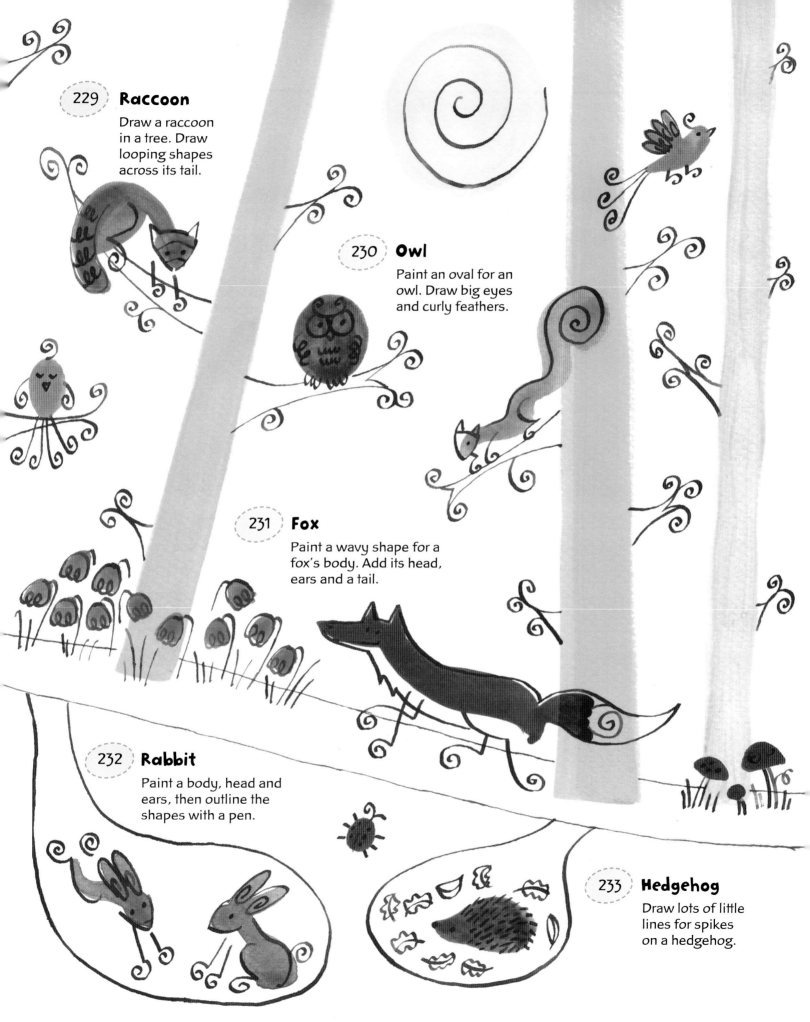

229 Raccoon

Draw a raccoon in a tree. Draw looping shapes across its tail.

230 Owl

Paint an oval for an owl. Draw big eyes and curly feathers.

231 Fox

Paint a wavy shape for a fox's body. Add its head, ears and a tail.

232 Rabbit

Paint a body, head and ears, then outline the shapes with a pen.

233 Hedgehog

Draw lots of little lines for spikes on a hedgehog.

Layered town painting

This town is painted on several strips of cardboard that are glued together to make one big 3-D picture.

234 **Build a town**

1. For the bottom street in the town, cut a strip of cardboard. Then, draw a line across it and add lots of houses and trees.

2. Cut around the trees and roofs of the houses, leaving a thin border. Then, lay the street on another piece of cardboard.

3. Draw a line along this strip, then add houses. Cut around them, too. Lay this on some cardboard and add more buildings.

4. Fill in all the shapes with different shades of paint. When the paint is dry, draw around the outlines with a felt-tip pen.

Pieces of cardboard

5. To build the town, cut squares of thick cardboard. Glue them along the bottom of the strips, then glue the strips on top of each other.

235 **Bricks**

Draw or paint bricks on the walls of some of the buildings.

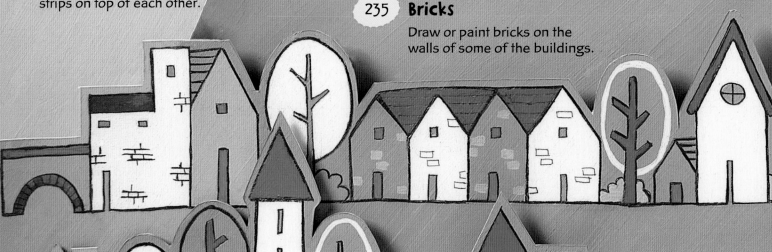

Hill

236 Draw a hill with some buildings and trees on top.

You could add an arch onto the side of a building.

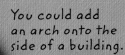

237 Castle
Draw a castle towering over the town. Add turrets, windows and a doorway.

238 Windmill
Draw the building, then add windows and sails.

Try drawing or painting tiles on the roofs of some of the buildings.

Drawing robots

Use the ideas on these pages to create lots of different robots. Start with the basic shapes below.

239

Basic head shapes

Draw one of these shapes for your robot's head, or design one of your own.

Draw this shape for a side-on head.

240

Try tubes for arms or legs.

Make the body from two or more shapes.

Basic body parts

Combine these shapes to 'build' a robot. Draw circles for joints.

Use this shape for shoulders.

You could draw an antenna on the head.

241

Thick outline

Draw a robot with a thin black pen. Then, go over the outline again to make a thicker outline.

242

Flying robot

Draw a robot with a turbo charger instead of legs.

243

Kneeling robot

Draw a bent leg with a 'hinge' for a knee.

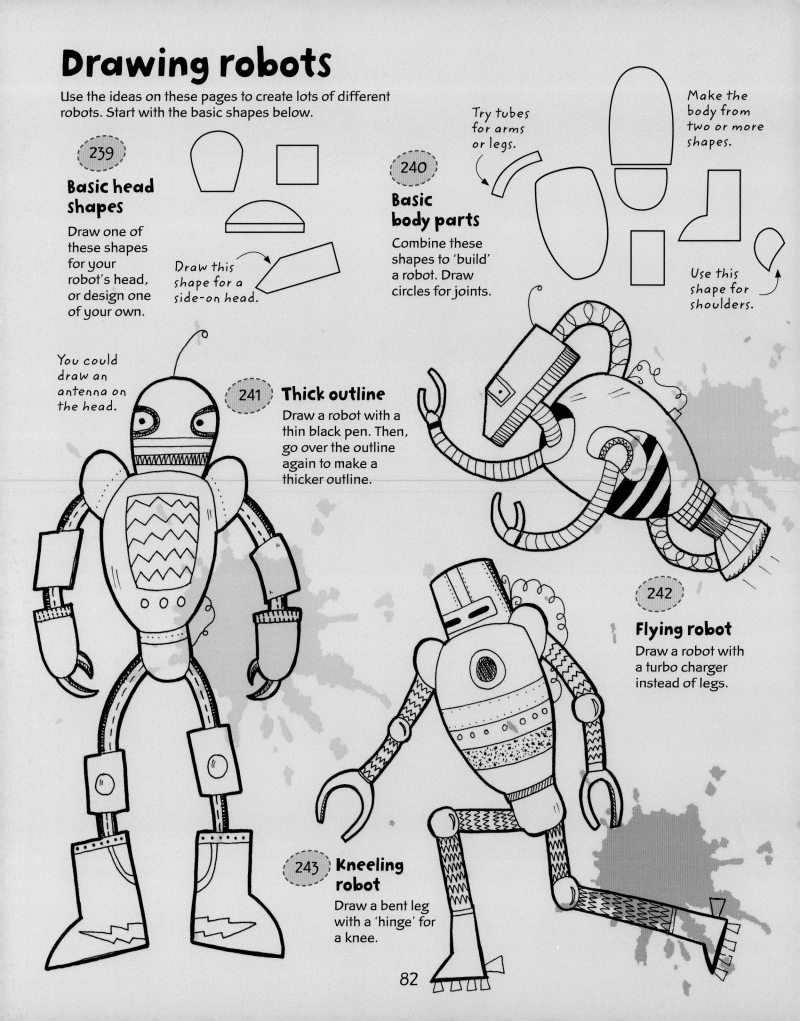

82

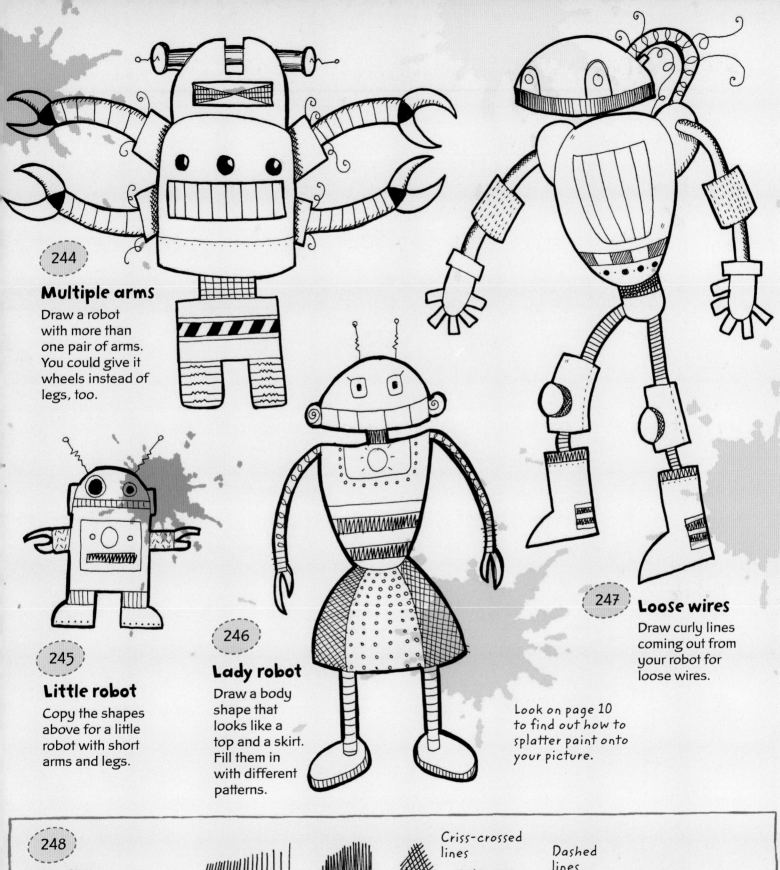

244

Multiple arms

Draw a robot with more than one pair of arms. You could give it wheels instead of legs, too.

245

Little robot

Copy the shapes above for a little robot with short arms and legs.

246

Lady robot

Draw a body shape that looks like a top and a skirt. Fill them in with different patterns.

247

Loose wires

Draw curly lines coming out from your robot for loose wires.

Look on page 10 to find out how to splatter paint onto your picture.

248

Shading techniques

Here are a few ideas for ways of filling in parts of a robot. Draw them with a thin pen.

Lines with different spaces between them.

Zigzags

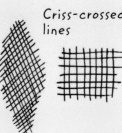

Criss-crossed lines

Dashed lines

Spots

Flower girls

249 Simple flower girl

Add cheeks with a pink pencil.

Draw little shoes, too.

1. Use a thin black felt-tip pen to draw the head, face and neck. Then, add the hair and cheeks.

2. Draw the body and fill it in. Then, add an arm stretched out on either side of the body. Add legs.

3. Look in old magazines for a photo of a flower. Cut out the petals and glue them on as a skirt.

4. Draw a flower, stem and leaf beneath one of the girl's feet. Then, draw another flower beside it.

250 Flower garden

Make a big picture with lots of flower girls in a garden. Draw some flowers and add photos of flowers, too.

251 Headdress

Cut out individual petals or leaves and glue them on as a headdress.

84

This hat is the head of a poppy seed.

You could draw pointed high-heeled boots instead of shoes.

252 **Flowery hat**

Use a photo of a flower as a hat. Trim some of the petals so that they don't cover the face.

253 **Tissue paper skirt**

Cut petals from tissue paper and glue them on overlapping each other.

Penguins on the ice

Follow the steps to paint an icy background, then fill it with lots of penguins having fun on the ice.

254 **Icy background**

Some paint will seep into the creases.

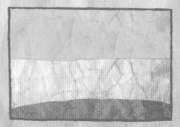

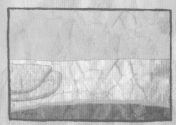

1. Draw all over a piece of white paper with a white wax crayon or a white candle. Then, scrunch the paper into a tight ball.

2. Flatten the paper and paint it all over with blue paint. Then, rinse the paper under cold running water, rubbing it gently.

3. Leave the paper to dry. Then, draw a line for the horizon and another line for the sea. Fill the sky and sea with blue paints.

4. Paint another line along the edge of the sea. Draw some curved lines for blocks on the ice and paint them, too.

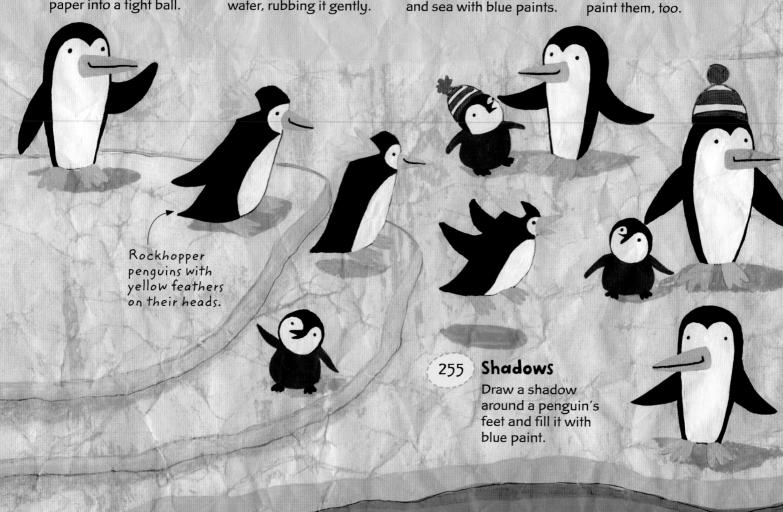

Rockhopper penguins with yellow feathers on their heads.

255 **Shadows**
Draw a shadow around a penguin's feet and fill it with blue paint.

256 **Swimming penguins**
Draw a penguin in the sea and paint it with thick paint.

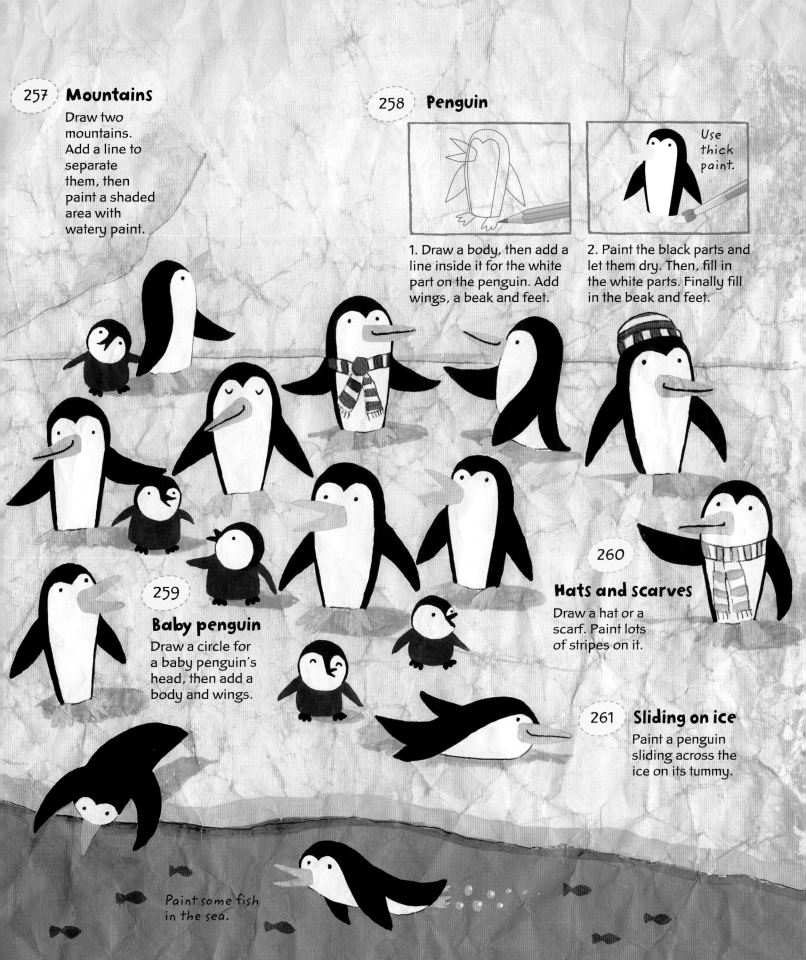

257 **Mountains**
Draw two mountains. Add a line to separate them, then paint a shaded area with watery paint.

258 **Penguin**

Use thick paint.

1. Draw a body, then add a line inside it for the white part on the penguin. Add wings, a beak and feet.

2. Paint the black parts and let them dry. Then, fill in the white parts. Finally fill in the beak and feet.

259

Baby penguin
Draw a circle for a baby penguin's head, then add a body and wings.

260

Hats and scarves
Draw a hat or a scarf. Paint lots of stripes on it.

261 **Sliding on ice**
Paint a penguin sliding across the ice on its tummy.

Paint some fish in the sea.

Printed fruit and vegetables

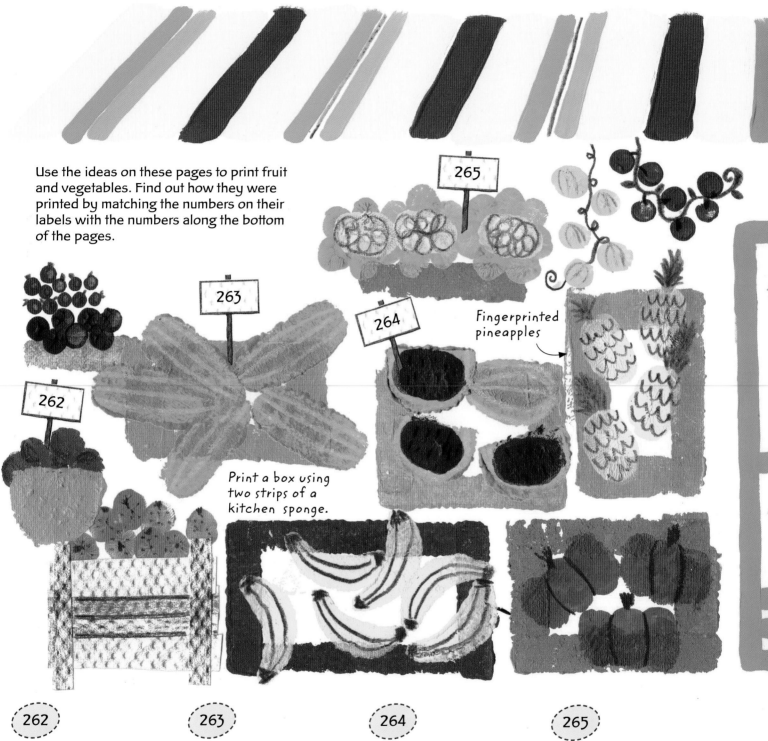

Use the ideas on these pages to print fruit and vegetables. Find out how they were printed by matching the numbers on their labels with the numbers along the bottom of the pages.

265

263

264

262

Fingerprinted pineapples

Print a box using two strips of a kitchen sponge.

262

Potatoes

Dip a fingertip into brown paint, then print it several times. When the paint is dry, print a bowl with a piece of a kitchen sponge.

263

Marrow

Cut a long oval from a piece of a sponge. Dip it into green paint, then print it. Draw lines with a white pencil when the paint is dry.

264

Watermelon slice

Cut a 'D' shape from a piece of a sponge. Print it with bright green paint. Do a red fingerprint on each shape. Then, draw seeds and white lines.

265

Cauliflower

Do green fingerprints for the leaves. When the paint is dry, fingerprint white spots. Then, draw looping shapes on top.

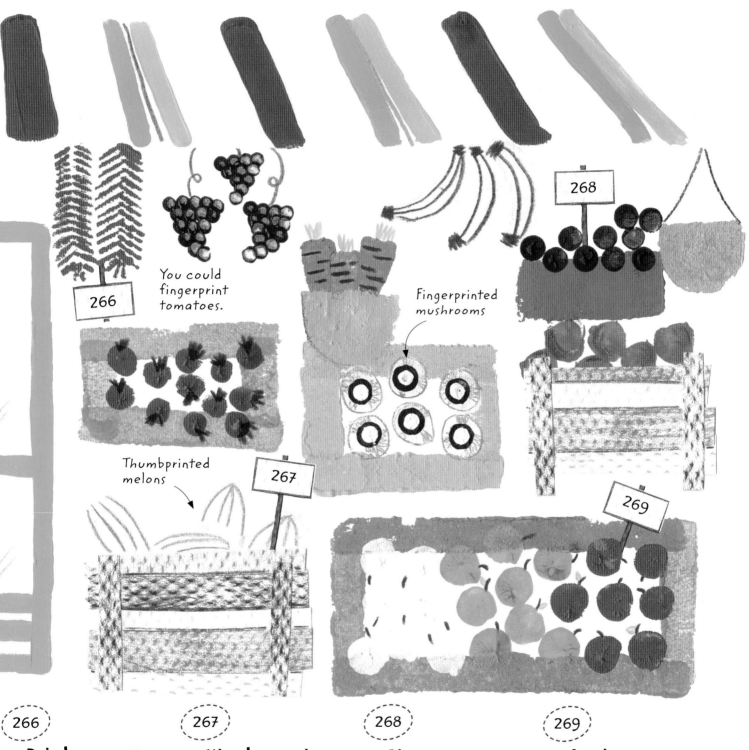

You could fingerprint tomatoes.

Fingerprinted mushrooms

Thumbprinted melons

266

267

268

269

266
Dried peppers
Dip a thin paintbrush into red paint. Then, use the side of the bristles to print lots of little diagonal lines for strings of peppers.

267
Wooden crate
Lay a piece of paper over the fine holes on a cheese grater and rub a wax crayon over it. Then, cut the paper into strips to make a crate.

268
Plums
Use a piece of sponge to print a box. Then, dip the tip of your little finger into dark purple paint. Dab it lightly on your paper for plums.

269
Apples
Print a box with pieces of a kitchen sponge. When the paint is dry, fingerprint apples. Then, draw stalks with a brown pencil.

Patterned park

1. Draw a tree trunk and branches with an oil pastel in the middle of a piece of paper. Then, add lots of flowers with a pencil.

2. Use pencils to draw leaves among the flowers, and on the branches. Fill in all the shapes with different pastels.

3. Then, look at the ideas on these pages and add a smaller tree, and lots of patterned bushes and flowers to your picture.

270 Fruit tree

Use a pale pastel to draw the top and trunk of a tree. Then, use pencils to fill the top with leaves and flowers, and round shapes for fruit.

271 Shadow flowers

Use a dark pastel to draw flowers, leaves and stems to make them look as if they are in the shadows of the other plants.

90

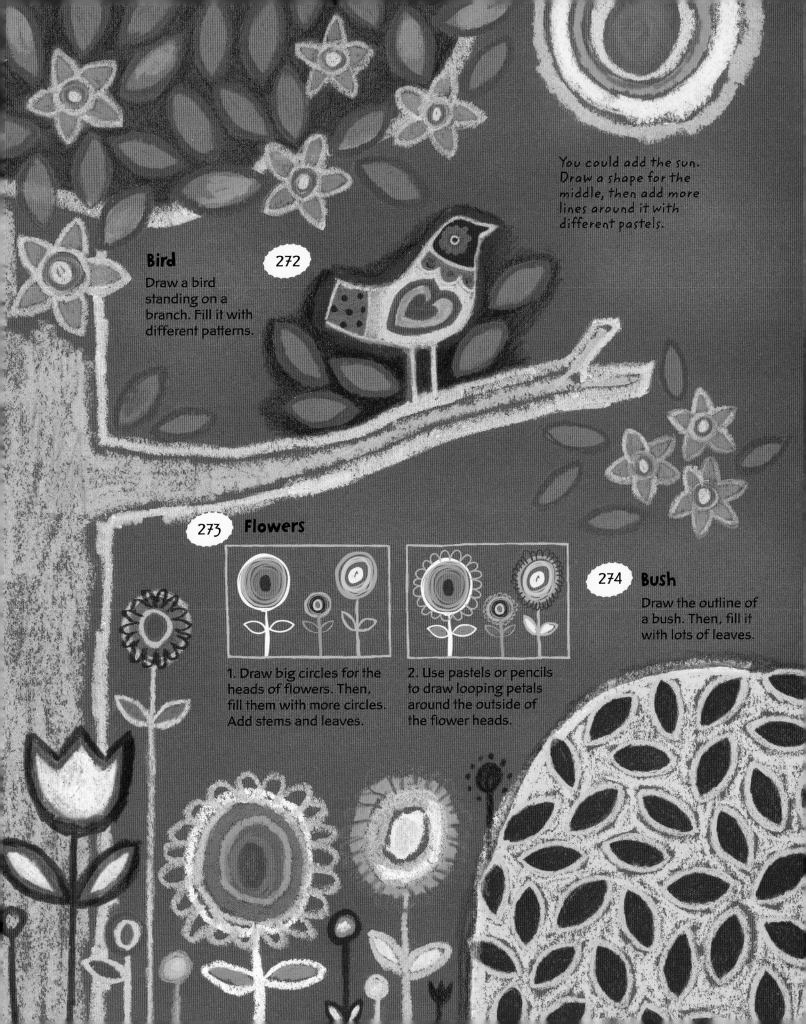

You could add the sun. Draw a shape for the middle, then add more lines around it with different pastels.

Bird

272

Draw a bird standing on a branch. Fill it with different patterns.

273 **Flowers**

1. Draw big circles for the heads of flowers. Then, fill them with more circles. Add stems and leaves.

2. Use pastels or pencils to draw looping petals around the outside of the flower heads.

274 **Bush**

Draw the outline of a bush. Then, fill it with lots of leaves.

(276) **Crown**

Cut a crown from paper and glue it on.

Dancing princesses

(275) **Princess**

Use a thin brush.

1. Draw the top of a dress on red paper. Cut it out and glue it onto darker paper. Cut out a skirt. Add another layer at the bottom.

2. Draw a neck, head and face. Add hair flowing out to one side. Then, draw sleeves and hands stretching out to the sides.

3. Paint her head, neck and hands. When the paint is dry, fill in her eyelids and lips. Then, paint her sleeves.

4. Paint dainty feet and little slippers. Then, add lots of dots all over her skirt using a thin brush and thick white paint.

277 Zigzag pattern

Cut lots of triangles along the edge of one of the layers of the skirt.

Try painting a sash, too.

The window and the line for the edge of the room was added after the princesses were glued onto the paper.

You could decorate the skirt with flowers cut from paper.

278 Dots and crosses

Paint lots of crosses and dots on the layers of the skirt. Add stripes to the bottom layer.

Cups and plates collage

Use the ideas on these pages to make a collage with stacks of patterned cups, plates, bowls and teapots.

Make lots of cups and glue them onto another piece of paper.

1. Draw the outline of a cup on a piece of paper. Use pencils to decorate it with lots of patterns.

2. Very carefully cut out the hole in the handle with a craft knife. Then, use scissors to cut out the cup.

Try combining different patterns on each cup.

279 Saucer

Cut a strip of thin paper and cut a curve at each end. Glue it below a cup.

280 Spoon

Draw the handle of a spoon on some kitchen foil and glue it poking out above the rim of a cup.

You could add little cupcakes in paper cases.

281 **Bowls**

Draw a bowl and decorate it. Cut it out and add it to your collage.

Try decorating the objects with wavy patterns.

282 **Teapots**

Draw a teapot or a coffee pot with a handle, lid and a spout.

You could decorate a coffee pot with circles and stripes.

Jungle silhouette

Use the ideas on these pages to paint a silhouette of animals, plants and birds in a jungle. Use a thick paintbrush to paint the larger shapes and a thinner one to add smaller details.

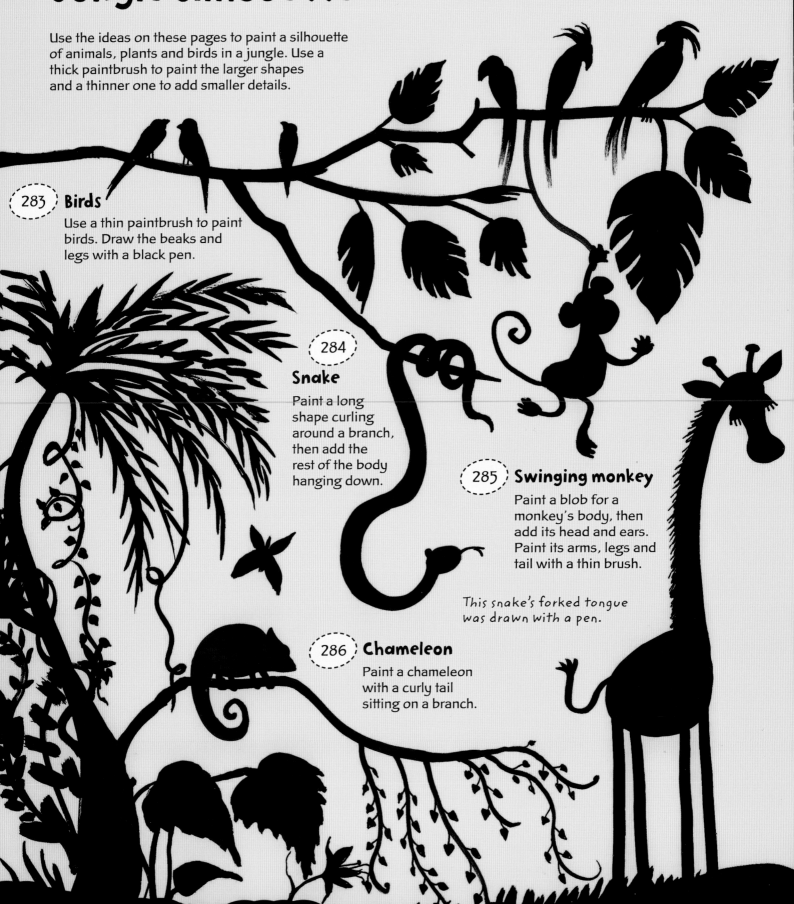

(283) Birds

Use a thin paintbrush to paint birds. Draw the beaks and legs with a black pen.

(284) Snake

Paint a long shape curling around a branch, then add the rest of the body hanging down.

(285) Swinging monkey

Paint a blob for a monkey's body, then add its head and ears. Paint its arms, legs and tail with a thin brush.

This snake's forked tongue was drawn with a pen.

(286) Chameleon

Paint a chameleon with a curly tail sitting on a branch.

287
Vines

Paint a thin line
for a vine. Then,
use the tip of the
brush to add lots
of leaves on either
side of the line.

You could
paint a lizard
sitting on a
branch.

Paint some
butterflies
fluttering
in the sky.

288 **Giraffe**

Copy the shapes shown
here to paint a giraffe with
a curving neck, oval body
and long, thin legs.

Windy day painting

289 Painting the scene

1. Use a pencil to draw a line curving across a piece of paper. Add shapes for the trunks of two trees.

2. Draw lines for the branches, making them bend over to one side. Add lots of leaves.

3. Draw a washing line between the trees. Add another one going off the side of the paper.

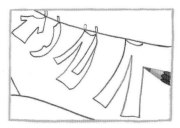

4. Draw clothes hanging on the line, making them 'fly' as if they are being blown by the wind.

You could draw stripes on the girl's hat with a pencil.

291 Kite

Draw a kite with a long tail blowing in the wind. Paint it with bright paints.

290 Grass

Paint lots of brushstrokes for blades of long grass.

5. Draw a hat, then the head of a girl. Add her hair, and a dress blowing in front of her.

6. Draw her arms stretched out in front of her, too. Add her legs. Then, draw an umbrella turned inside out.

7. Fill in the picture with watery paints. Paint patterns on the clothes and on the girl's dress.

8. When the paint is completely dry, go over all the pencil lines with a thin black felt-tip pen.

292 **Clouds**

Paint several clouds in the sky with watery blue paint.

293 **Leaves**

Add some leaves blowing in the wind.

You could add a pole propping up the line.

99

Traffic jam

Copy the ideas on these pages to draw a scene filled with roads, cars and other vehicles. Start by drawing the roads.

294 **Cars**

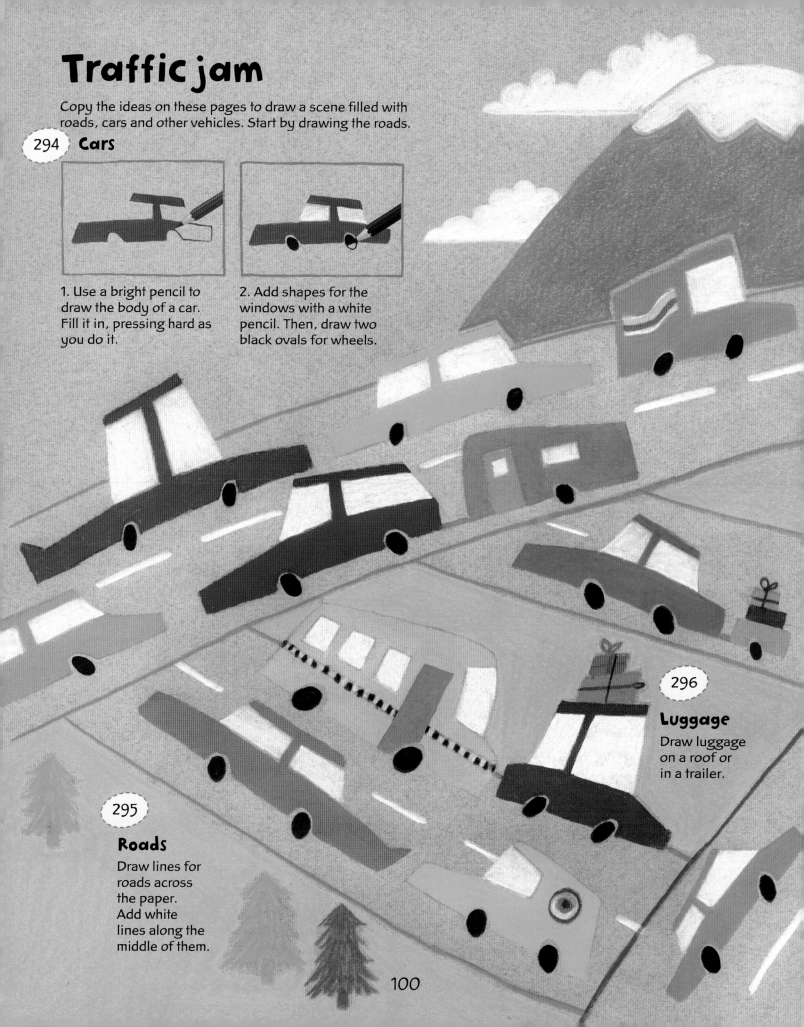

1. Use a bright pencil to draw the body of a car. Fill it in, pressing hard as you do it.

2. Add shapes for the windows with a white pencil. Then, draw two black ovals for wheels.

296

Luggage
Draw luggage on a roof or in a trailer.

295

Roads
Draw lines for roads across the paper. Add white lines along the middle of them.

297 Mountains
Use purple pencils to draw mountains in the distance.

298 Boat
Draw a boat on a trailer behind a car.

299 Trees
Draw trees between the roads. Fill in around them with a light green pencil.

Trapeze artists

The figures on this page were drawn with a black ballpoint pen, so that you can paint over the lines without the ink running. You could also use a felt-tip pen that has permanent ink.

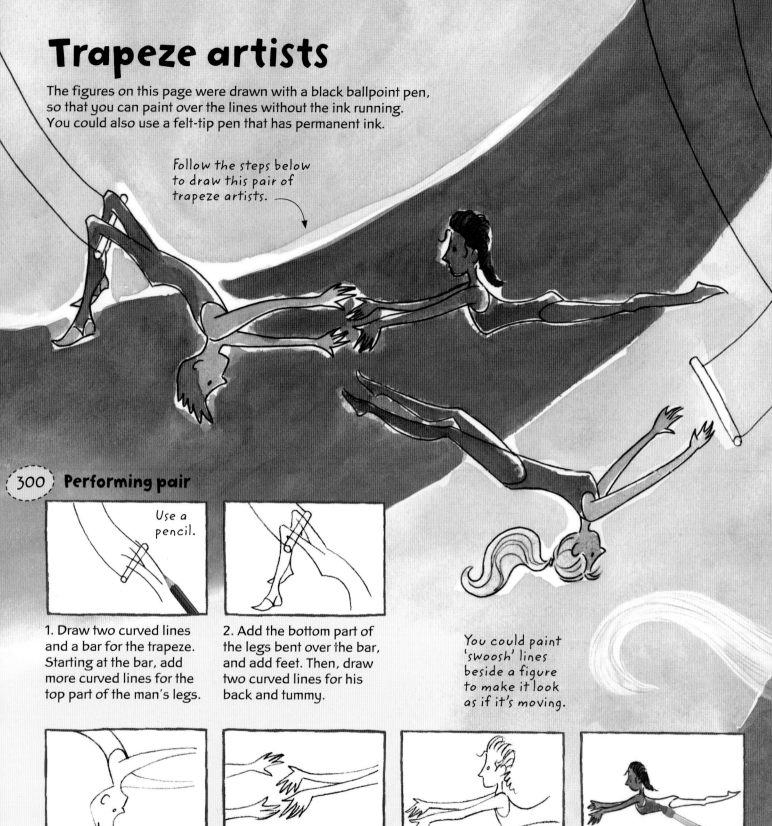

Follow the steps below to draw this pair of trapeze artists.

You could paint 'swoosh' lines beside a figure to make it look as if it's moving.

300 **Performing pair**

Use a pencil.

1. Draw two curved lines and a bar for the trapeze. Starting at the bar, add more curved lines for the top part of the man's legs.

2. Add the bottom part of the legs bent over the bar, and add feet. Then, draw two curved lines for his back and tummy.

3. Draw a neck and head, and add some hair, an ear and an eye. Then, add the arms and a curve for the top of his outfit.

4. Draw a hand on the end of the man's arms. Then, draw another pair of outstretched hands and arms next to them.

5. Draw the tops of the girl's arms. Add her neck and head, her hair, an ear and an eye. Draw curves for her back and tummy.

6. Add straight legs and feet with pointed toes. Draw over the pencil lines with a black ballpoint pen. Then, paint the figures.

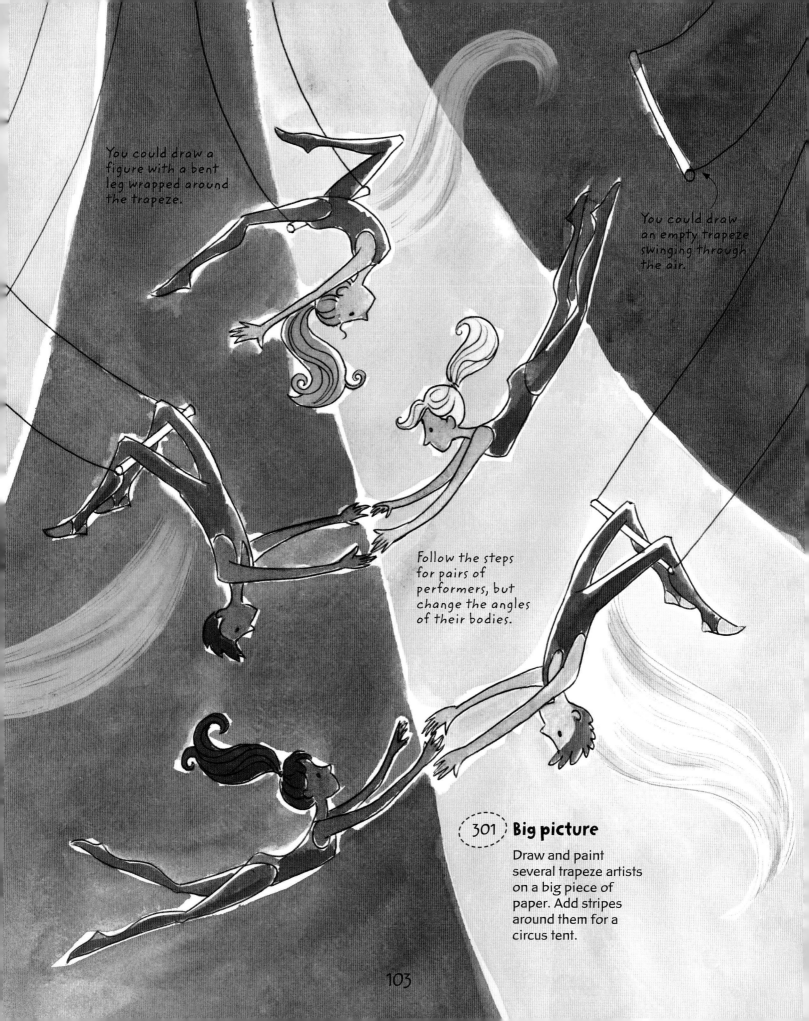

You could draw a figure with a bent leg wrapped around the trapeze.

You could draw an empty trapeze swinging through the air.

Follow the steps for pairs of performers, but change the angles of their bodies.

301 **Big picture**

Draw and paint several trapeze artists on a big piece of paper. Add stripes around them for a circus tent.

Painted parrots

302 Red parrot

You don't need to be too neat.

1. Dip a fingertip into some thick red paint and print a shape for the parrot's head on a piece of paper.

2. Fingerpaint an oval for the body. Drag your finger across the paper to make the wings and tail feathers.

3. Then, fingerpaint a white patch on one side of the head. Leave the paint to dry completely.

4. Use a black pen to add the eye, feet and beak. Then, draw green wing feathers with chalk.

Use the ideas shown here to draw different shapes of birds and cages.

303 Lovebirds

Fingerpaint two birds, then draw a cage around them. Draw a perch for each one.

Fingerpaint a bird perching on a cage.

306 Bird in a cage

1. Use a thin black pen to draw a rectangle around a painted bird. Then, draw lines for the bars.

Add a perch, too.

2. Add another line along the top and bottom of the cage. Then, draw curved lines for the top of it.

304 Pointed beak

Fingerpaint a head, body and wings of a flycatcher, then add a small eye and a long beak.

305 Flying parrot

Fingerpaint the wings stretched out above the parrot's body. Use more than one shade of paint.

Vegetable monsters

307 **Vegetable prints**

1. Put your vegetable on a chopping board, then cut across it very carefully with a sharp knife. Try to cut through it in one cut.

2. Spread some thick paint onto an old plate. Then, press the cut side of the vegetable into the paint to cover the surface.

3. Press the vegetable onto a piece of paper to print the shape. Make more prints and leave them to dry.

4. Turn the shape into a monster by drawing arms and legs with a felt-tip pen. Add teeth and eyes with a pen or paint.

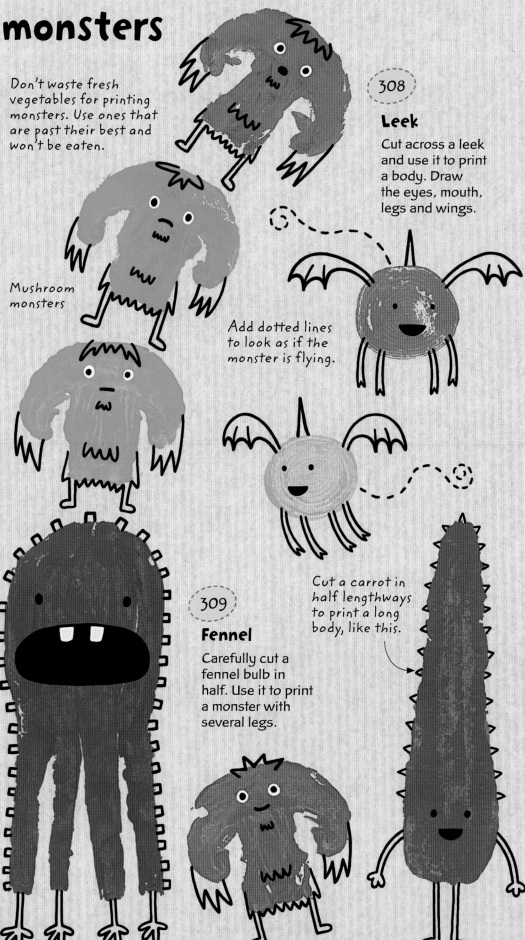

Don't waste fresh vegetables for printing monsters. Use ones that are past their best and won't be eaten.

Mushroom monsters

308

Leek

Cut across a leek and use it to print a body. Draw the eyes, mouth, legs and wings.

Add dotted lines to look as if the monster is flying.

309

Fennel

Carefully cut a fennel bulb in half. Use it to print a monster with several legs.

Cut a carrot in half lengthways to print a long body, like this.

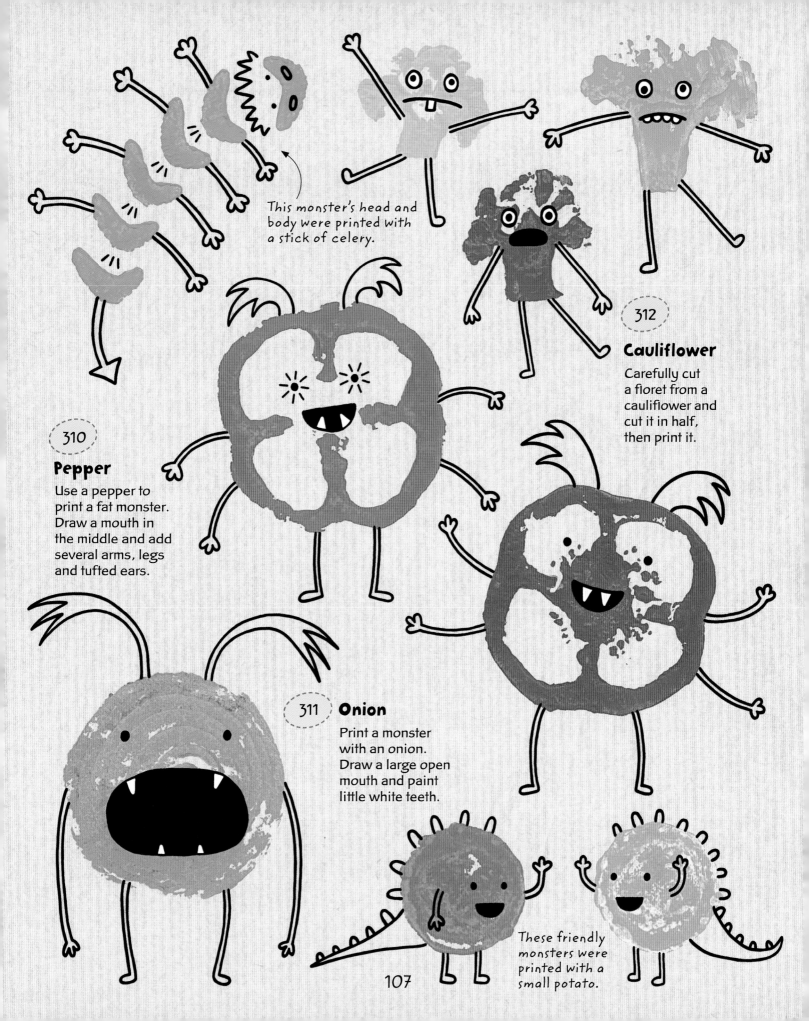

This monster's head and body were printed with a stick of celery.

312

Cauliflower

Carefully cut a floret from a cauliflower and cut it in half, then print it.

310

Pepper

Use a pepper to print a fat monster. Draw a mouth in the middle and add several arms, legs and tufted ears.

311 **Onion**

Print a monster with an onion. Draw a large open mouth and paint little white teeth.

These friendly monsters were printed with a small potato.

Safari picture

313 **Leopard in a tree**

Add some leaves.

Paint spots on the leopard, too.

1. Paint a branch and tree trunk with orange paint or ink on brown paper. Paint around the edge of the paper, too. Let it dry.

2. Draw a leopard lying on top of the branch. Then, go over all the lines with dark brown paint or ink. Leave it to dry.

3. Fill in the leopard with pencils. Add some shading, and draw around some of the painted spots.

315 **Grasses**

Add grasses in the background with orange and pale green paints.

314 **Zebra**

Copy the outline of one of the zebras above, then add a mane and a tail. Paint black lines on the body and fill in between them with pencils.

You could scribble shadows under the animals with a brown pencil.

This blue shading in the sky was drawn with a chalk pastel, then smudged a little.

You could draw some birds on the branches of the tree.

316 Lion

Draw a sleeping lion or one roaring with its mouth open. Use an orange pencil to draw thin lines on the mane.

Hearts and flowers

All the hearts and flowers on these pages were painted with thick paint, then details were added with a felt-tip pen when the paint had dried.

317

Hearts in hearts

Paint a pink heart, then add a purple one inside it. Fill this heart with smaller heart shapes.

318 **Petals**

Paint individual flower petals around a circle. Then, paint a larger flower shape around them.

Try painting dots and lines.

Draw lines to look like stitching.

You could paint a heart in each petal of a flower.

319 **Spiral patterns**
Paint lots of circles of different sizes in the middle of a flower. Draw spirals on top.

These dots were drawn on the heart first, then the lines were added.

Football crowd

320 Draw a crowd

To do a crowd of supporters, start by painting a row of heads and bodies at the bottom of your paper. Then, draw more rows of people above.

Use the ideas shown here to draw different smiles on the happy fans.

321 Happy fan

1. Mix a watery skin tone using orange and pink paint. Then, paint a rough oval shape for a head.

322 Waving a scarf

Paint two lines for arms and add blobs for the stripes on a scarf.

2. Paint an oval for a body beneath the head, using a different shade of watery paint.

323 Cheering fan

Draw a huge oval for a mouth, and add little teeth.

You could draw an oval mouth for a surprised expression.

3. Paint a blob for the hair. It doesn't matter if the paint runs into the face a little.

324 Punching the air

Paint a line for a raised arm coming from the shoulder.

4. When the paint is dry, draw a line around the bottom of the face. Then, add some ears.

5. Draw dots for the eyes. Then, add a mouth and nose, and some curly lines in the hair.

6. Draw a scarf. Then, add curved lines for the shoulders, and two short lines for arms.

You could draw two groups of fans. Make one group unhappy because their team is losing.

Use some of the expressions shown here for unhappy fans.

(325) **Striped scarf**

Paint stripes, then add blobs for the body around them.

(326) **Hats**

Draw a hat instead of adding hair.

(327) **Hands on head**

Paint arms on either side of the head, and add hands.

Superheroes

The steps on this page shows you how to build up shapes to create cartoon superheroes. Once you have drawn them use the ideas on the opposite page to add clothes.

328 **Male body shape**

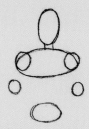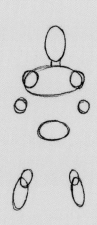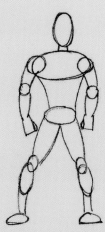

1. Draw an oval for a head. Add a neck, and larger ovals for the shoulders and hips. Draw circles in the shoulders, and add elbows.

2. Draw two ovals for knees beneath the hips. Then, add two longer ovals for the superhero's calf muscles.

3. Add squares for hands and draw ovals for the thumbs. Then, join all the shapes together like this, and add feet.

4. Draw around the outlines with a felt-tip pen, adding ears to the head as you do it. Then, erase the pencil lines.

329 **Female body shape**

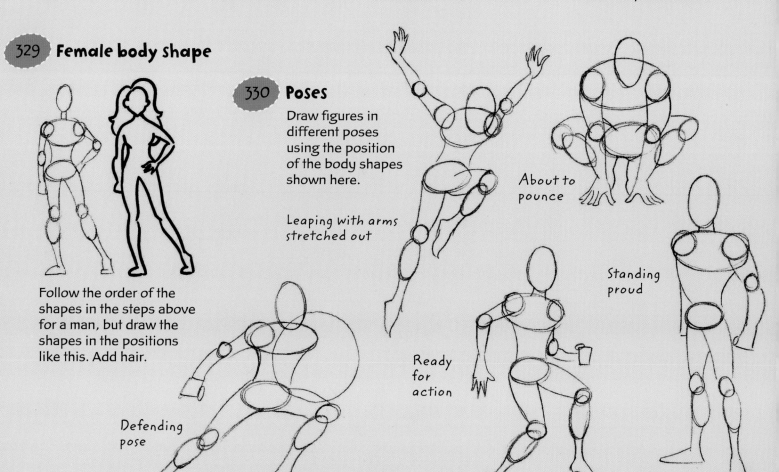

Follow the order of the shapes in the steps above for a man, but draw the shapes in the positions like this. Add hair.

330 **Poses**

Draw figures in different poses using the position of the body shapes shown here.

Leaping with arms stretched out

About to pounce

Defending pose

Ready for action

Standing proud

114

331 Movement lines

Draw lines beside the body to make the figure look as if it's moving.

332 Outfits

Use the ideas shown here for superheroes' clothes. Draw them before you draw the outline around the figure - see step 4 on the opposite page.

Add a cape with a collar.

Add a mask, shoulder protectors and a belt.

Draw large gloves.

You could draw simple boots or boots with the top folded over, like this one.

Decorated elephants

333 Draw an elephant

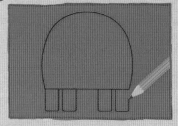 

1. Draw a curved hump for the elephant's back on a piece of thick paper. Draw four legs, too.

2. Draw a trunk and mouth. Cut out the shape, then erase the pencil lines. Draw an ear and an eye.

334 Make a picture

Cut out a large elephant, and lots of leaves and flowers from paper. Glue them onto another piece of paper, then use the ideas on these pages to decorate them.

335 Patterned elephant

Draw patterns on the elephant's trunk, ear and body. Add toenails, and patterns on the legs, too.

336 Flowery elephant

Draw some flowers curling up the elephant's legs. Add a big flower on its body.

337 Blanket

Draw a blanket on the elephant's back and a triangle on the head. Decorate them with patterns.

338 Baby elephant

Draw and cut out a mother elephant. Then, draw a smaller one for a baby. Glue it onto the mother.

339 **Bird**
Cut out a bird's body
and wings from paper
and glue them onto your
picture. Then, add an
eye and lots of patterns.

You could draw a
flower's stem with a
pen, then add lots of
patterns to the petals
and the leaves.

Soapy flamingos

If you mix watery paint with soap, you can see the brushed lines when the paint has dried.

(340) Flamingo

1. Dip a brush with stiff bristles into watery pink paint. Then, move the bristles around on an old bar of soap.

2. Brush a back-to-front 'S' shape for the flamingo's neck. Then, paint the head, and brush several curved lines for the body.

3. When the paint is dry, draw long, thin legs with a black felt-tip pen. Add a beak and fill in the end of it. Draw an eye, too.

(341) Water
Use different shades of soapy blue paint to brush horizontal lines for water

(342) Legs and feet
Draw a bent leg and add three lines for a flamingo's foot.

118

343 Clouds
Use soapy pale blue paint to add clouds in the sky.

Draw the legs of a flying flamingo stretched out behind the body.

346 Stork
Follow the instructions for the flamingo, using white paint for the body. Paint black tail feathers, and draw a red beak and legs.

344 Flying flamingo
Paint the body first, then do long brushstrokes for wings and neck.

Paint lines for reeds with the tip of a thin paintbrush.

345
Sandy bank
Paint a sandy bank with light brown soapy paint. Add birds standing on it.

119

Painted dragon

347 **Draw and paint a dragon**

Follow the step-by-step instructions along the bottom of the pages to draw and paint the dragon. You will need a long piece of paper.

348 **Fire**

Use shades of orange paint to add flames. Draw over the top with a pencil when the paint is dry.

349 **Paper scales**

Cut out scales from paper and glue them along the dragon's body.

1. Use a pencil to draw shapes like these for the dragon's jaws at one end of a long piece of paper.

2. Add nostrils, ears and large eyes with eyelashes. Then, draw a frill around the back of the head.

3. Draw a neck. Then, add a long, wavy shape for the body, making it thinner at the tail.

4. Add four short legs with feet. Then, draw curved claws. Draw flame shapes at the end of the tail, too.

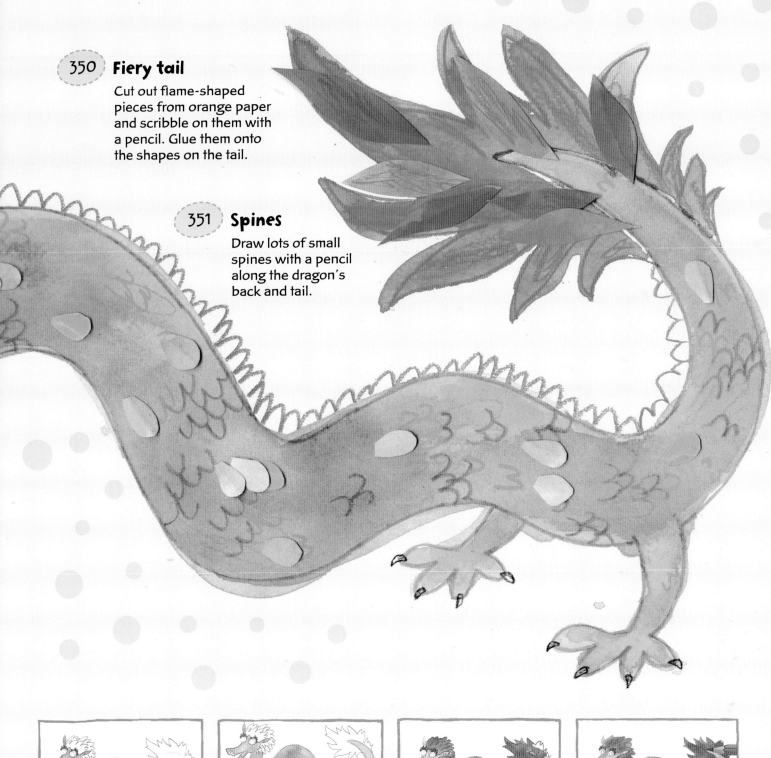

350 Fiery tail

Cut out flame-shaped pieces from orange paper and scribble on them with a pencil. Glue them onto the shapes on the tail.

351 Spines

Draw lots of small spines with a pencil along the dragon's back and tail.

5. Fill in the head and ears with watery blue paint. Then, paint the body with watery green paint.

The paints will bleed into each other.

6. Before the paint has had a chance to dry, paint some patches of blue paint onto the body, too.

7. Fill in the legs with green paint. Then, paint the frills on the head and tail with orange paint.

8. Paint the eyes yellow. Then, use pencils to add scales on the body. Draw flames on the frill and tail.

Tissue paper plants

All the plants on these pages were made from shapes ripped from tissue paper, glued onto paper, then decorated with pencils.

Try drawing spots on the leaves, too.

353

Tall palm

Rip shapes for the trunk and leaves. Draw lines and patterns on them.

352 **Fancy leaves**

Draw lines along the leaves. Then, add curly patterns, circles or ovals at the ends of the leaves.

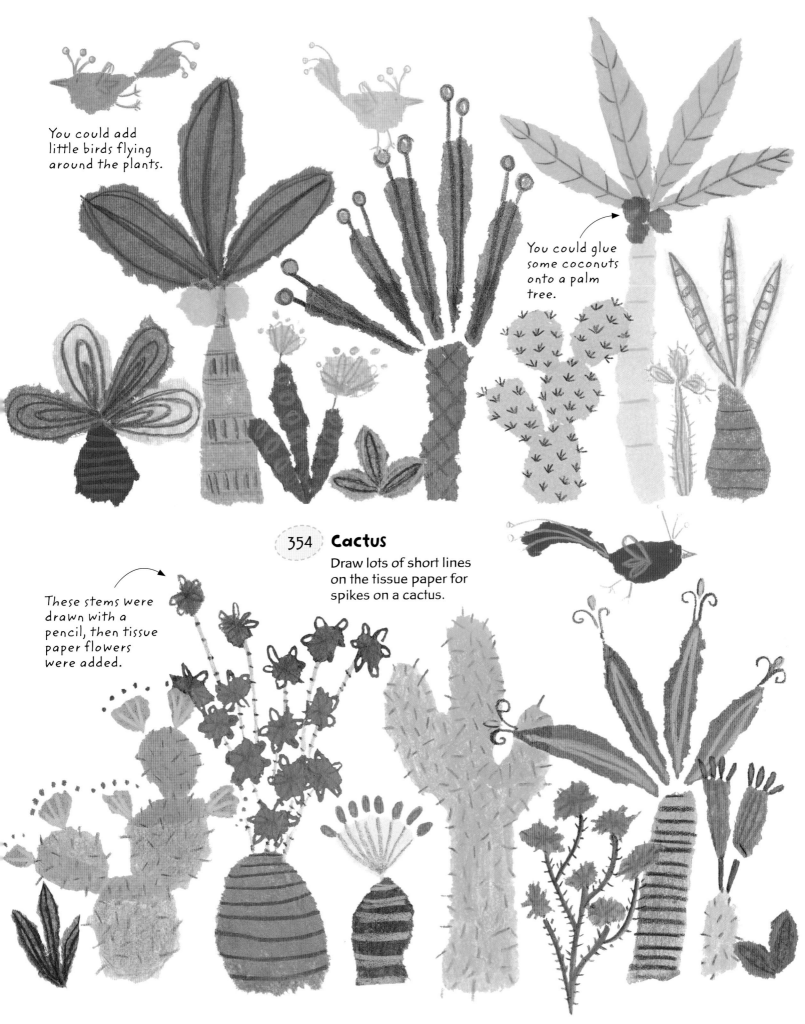

You could add little birds flying around the plants.

You could glue some coconuts onto a palm tree.

(354) **Cactus**
Draw lots of short lines on the tissue paper for spikes on a cactus.

These stems were drawn with a pencil, then tissue paper flowers were added.

Undersea doodle

Use pencils to doodle an underwater scene using the shapes and patterns on these pages for ideas.

356 **Sea horse**
Draw lots of little lines around a sea horse's eye and along its body.

355 **Big fish**
Draw a big fish. Doodle lines on the head and fins, and spirals on the body and tail.

Draw lots of wavy lines for seaweed.

359 **Octopus**
Draw an *octopus* with eight curling tentacles. Doodle patterns on its head, body and tentacles.

358 **Little fish**
Draw little fish swimming around the coral. Add eyes, and stripes on their bodies.

357 **Coral**
Draw coral in the corner of your picture. Fill it with wavy lines.

360 Jellyfish

Draw a jellyfish. Doodle lines on its body and tentacles.

Doodle lots of little circles for bubbles in the sea.

Rabbit burrow

Follow the steps to draw a large scene with lots of rabbits in a burrow, then fill it in with paints and pencils.

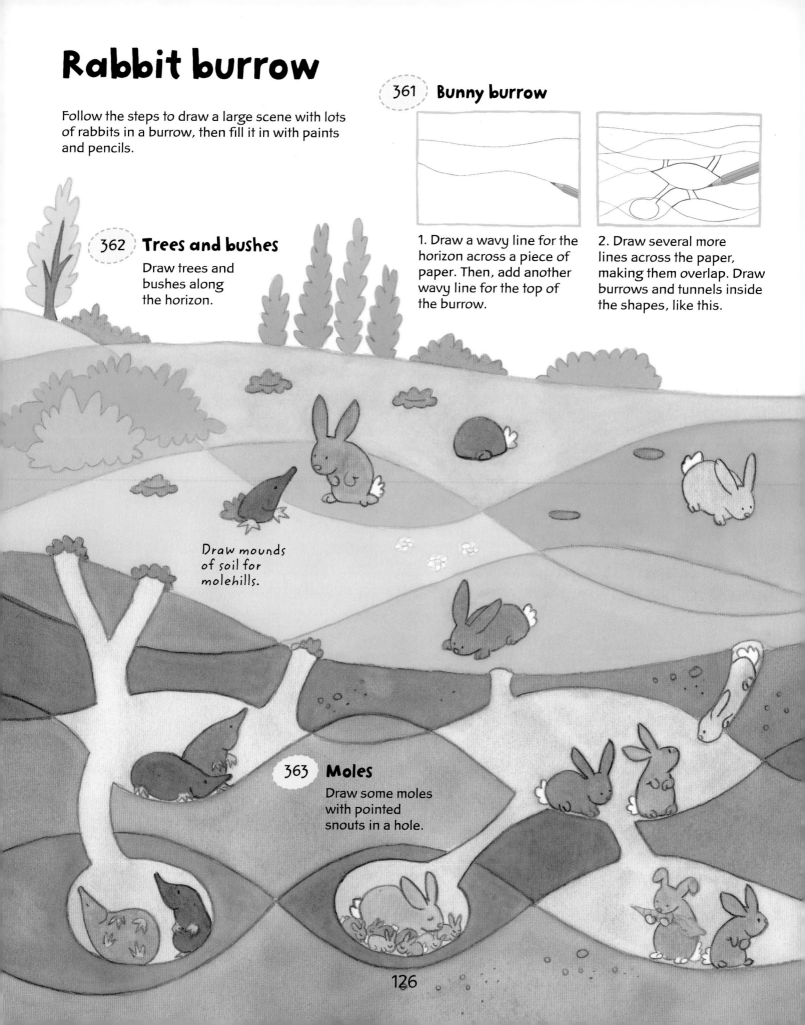

361 Bunny burrow

1. Draw a wavy line for the horizon across a piece of paper. Then, add another wavy line for the top of the burrow.

2. Draw several more lines across the paper, making them overlap. Draw burrows and tunnels inside the shapes, like this.

362 Trees and bushes

Draw trees and bushes along the horizon.

Draw mounds of soil for molehills.

363 Moles

Draw some moles with pointed snouts in a hole.

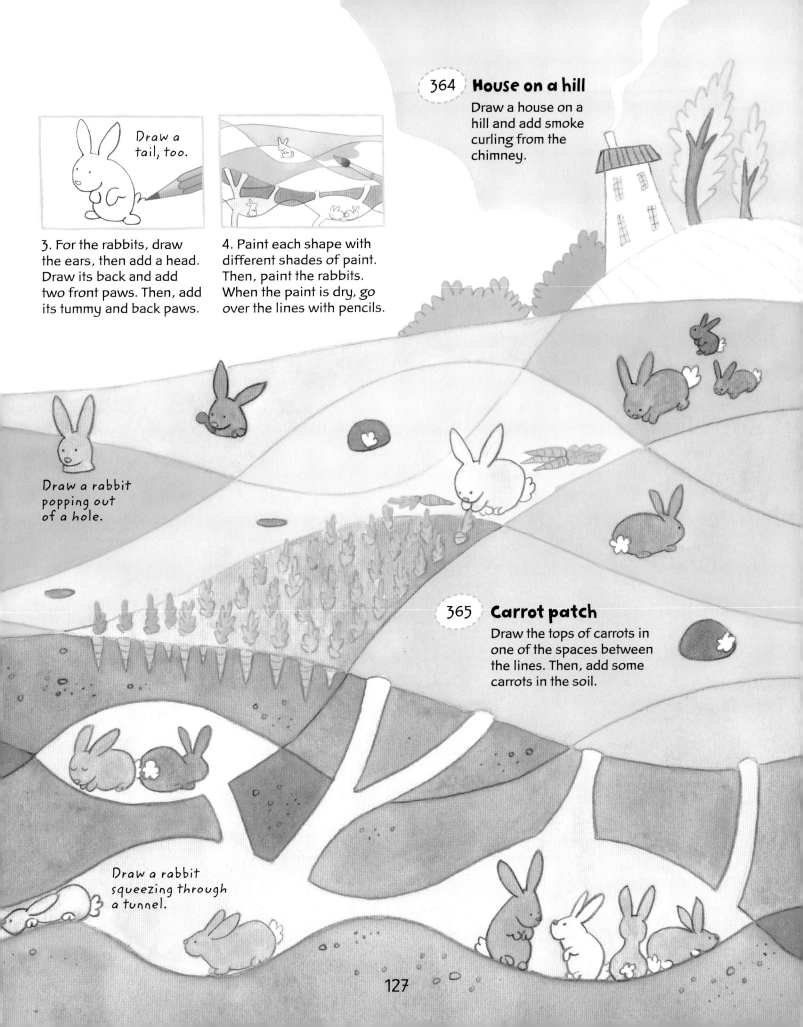

Draw a tail, too.

3. For the rabbits, draw the ears, then add a head. Draw its back and add two front paws. Then, add its tummy and back paws.

4. Paint each shape with different shades of paint. Then, paint the rabbits. When the paint is dry, go over the lines with pencils.

364 **House on a hill**
Draw a house on a hill and add smoke curling from the chimney.

Draw a rabbit popping out of a hole.

365 **Carrot patch**
Draw the tops of carrots in one of the spaces between the lines. Then, add some carrots in the soil.

Draw a rabbit squeezing through a tunnel.

... and if it's a leap year!

366 **Leaping grasshopper**

Paint a shape for the grasshopper's body. When the paint is dry, add its legs, eyes and feelers. Draw a mouth, and dots in the eyes.

Index

Photographs of flowers on pages 84-85 © Digital Vision
Photographic manipulation by John Russell · Photographs by Howard Allman
First published in 2009 by Usborne Publishing Ltd., Usborne House, 83-85 Saffron Hill, London, EC1N 8RT. www.usborne.com © 2009 Usborne Publishing
Ltd. The name Usborne and the devices ♀ ☺ are Trademarks of Usborne Publishing Ltd. All rights reserved. No part of this publication may be
reproduced, stored in a retrieval system or transmitted in any form or by any means, electronic, mechanical, photocopying, recording, or otherwise,
without previous permission of the publisher. UE First published in America 2011.